WILLIAM AND CATHERINE BOOTH:
GOD'S SOLDIERS

JENTY FAIRBANK

William and Catherine Booth: God's Soldiers

HODDER AND STOUGHTON
LONDON SYDNEY AUCKLAND TORONTO

Contents

Illustrations

I

CLOCKS CAN'T STRIKE THIRTEEN

'So I'm the *second* William Booth!' he whispered to himself in delight.

All of a sudden he began to feel a sense of importance creeping over him. After all, there couldn't be many thirteen-year-olds to whom it was given to make the enthralling discovery that they were following in the steps of an unknown elder brother *with exactly the same name*.

Lying wide-eyed in the darkness, William hugged himself with excitement. 'Nine, ten, eleven, twelve,' he counted in his head, as the church clock struck its way into his thinking. 'Clocks can't strike thirteen,' he murmured to himself. 'Just think what they're missing!'

It seemed to William, brimful of discovery as he was in that moment, thirteen was the beginning of everything. 'And people call it unlucky!' he chuckled into his pillow, remembering how his older sister, Ann, almost refused to put a foot outside the door when a Friday also happened to be the thirteenth day of the month. 'I wonder if *she* knows about the *first* William Booth?' He frowned at the darkness as it dawned upon him that this new and startling secret might, in the cold light of day, prove to be common knowledge. But no, Ann was, after all, only a girl; their father would never have taken her into his confidence in the way he had taken William.

'You're almost thirteen now, lad,' his father had said in a sudden burst of conversation that evening, quite taking William by surprise. It was his mother who usually remembered things like birthdays. His father was far too busy trying to think up ways of getting out of debt. 'Bankruptcy' was how the newspaper had described Samuel Booth's predicament, William remembered.

'Thirteen's a good age to think about the future, William. You can't stay at school for ever. In fact, I can't afford to keep you at school any longer, so I've found you employment.'

'Employment, Papa! Where?'

'On the corner of Goosegate — the pawn-broker's shop. You're to be an apprentice there for six years. Mr. Eames is the best pawnbroker in Nottingham, and he'll teach you all there is to know about the business.'

William had noticed the sadness in his mother's eyes. Often she looked sad these days. He hadn't time to give a second thought to it before his father was speaking again.

'I want you to make your way in the world and do well, lad. Your mother and I want to be proud of you, and we need your help in supporting the three

William Booth's birthplace

girls. After all, you're the only son in the family now.'

'*Now*, Papa? I've *always* been the only son!'

He saw his parents exchange glances.

'You'd better tell him, Samuel,' his mother had said.

And so it was that William had learnt about his father's first marriage nearly forty-five years before; of the two children of that marriage who had died in infancy; and of the *first* William Booth, also a son of that marriage, who had lived into his twenties and then died 'of consumption'.

'I wonder if *I'll* die "of consumption" before I'm twenty-five?' thought the half-asleep *second* William, shivering at the whole delicious mystery. 'Fancy there being two *Mrs.* Booths as well! One of them dead and one of them downstairs. That explains why Mama always seems so much younger than Papa; she's his *second* wife!'

'One!' struck the church clock that didn't know how to strike thirteen, and the almost-thirteen-year-old only son of the Booth family swam into a dreamless sleep.

2

THE DUKE AND THE TEA-LEAF CARRIER

The church clock was striking nine by the time William woke the next morning. It was a Saturday; even so, he could hear the stocking machines clattering noisily in the nearby factory.

He remembered having read a book at Mr. Bidulph's school describing the sort of conditions under which 'stockiners' had to work.

A man called William Cobbett wrote of folk who were 'uprooted from the countryside' because of the revolution occurring in farming methods, and were 'compelled to work fourteen hours a day, in a heat of eighty-four degrees, and liable to punishment for looking out at a window of the factory'!

'Thank goodness *I* shan't be working in any old stocking factory,' grinned William at the ceiling, reaching his long skinny arms towards it in a gigantic stretch and remembering that Mr. Bidulph's school was now behind him once and for all. 'The *second* William Booth will make his fortune in the pawnbroking trade!' he announced to the brass bed-knob on which his upside-down boot had perched all the night long.

Suddenly it dawned on him that he had but two days left before his fortune-making began. One-and-a-half days really, if he subtracted the time he'd spend at church tomorrow.

'I must find the gang and let them know the news,' he thought to himself as he groped under the bed for his other boot. 'I bet they'll wish it were them!'

The rest of the family had finished their scant breakfast long since — a fact brought home to William by the luke-warmness of the tea he gulped down, with his face screwed into a shudder of dis-taste. 'Ugh!' he gasped, as he grabbed the crusty end of the loaf and made for the street door. No further did he get, for there stood a frail, miserable-looking little woman, whose eyes pleaded their way into William's sensitive soul.

'Got any tea-leaves?' she whined pitifully. ''As your mother got any tea-leaves?'

His mother was already on her way to the market, he knew, and the others were nowhere about. There was nothing else for it; William would have to take the responsibility upon himself. Fetching the lidless teapot from the kitchen, he shook it over her outstretched hands until a dollop of wet tea-leaves fell into them.

'God bless you, son!' she whispered, and William saw there were tears in her tired eyes.

He was about to follow her down the street when he remembered his breakfast crust, abandoned on the kitchen table when he had gone to fetch the teapot. Quickly he crammed the bread into his mouth, tore another hunk from the loaf and dashed off, in his hurry bumping into 'Grandfather Page' from the smallware shop across the road.

'Now then, young fellah me lad . . .' protested the old man; but the culprit had already disappeared along one of the countless narrow alleyways which laced that part of Nottingham, making it a paradise of exploration for gangs such as his.

In no time at all his long legs caught up with the tea-leaf carrier and she cowered in fear as his long, dark shadow drew level with hers and stopped.

'It's all right, mother!' he said gently. 'Here's some bread to go with the tea.' Balancing the hunk of new-smelling bread on top of the handful of tea-leaves, he was off with the speed of a Robin Hood arrow.

The church clock struck a lazy ten as William reached the market place, and for a moment he paused in his wild chase, his eyes searching among the crowds for some sign of the gang. He spotted them, dancing along behind 'Besom Jack', the broom-seller, already quite drunk, early in the day though it was. William joined in the fun for a while, but since the whole of Nottingham knew Besom Jack to be a wife-beater and given to frequent bouts of violence, the first lash of a broom on young Francis Brown's legs sent the boys scuttling off in safer directions.

'Now Wellington's come we can play at soldiers!' Will Sansom shouted, snatching a stick from the gutter and 'fixing bayonets'. William laughed, proud of his nickname, though not always so proud of the long nose which earned him this comparison with the famous 'Iron Duke'. To have won the Battle of Waterloo in 1815, and to have helped in 'inventing' the Police Force as Prime Minister in 1829, was enough to make the Duke of Wellington any boy's hero.

'No! Let's play Peelers today,' William suggested, feeling a special affinity with the policemen named after Sir Robert Peel, because the force had officially come into being in the exact year he himself had been born.

'Well, you can still be Wellington; I'll be a Peeler; and Frankie, Walley and Boldie can be pickpockets,' decided Will Sansom. 'It's a perfect day for it, what with all these crowds.'

The three pickpockets lost themselves to view in no time at all; the Peeler pursued his beat with measured tread and watchful eye; the Duke of Wellington, hands clasped behind his back, made his impressive way through the Saturday crowds, bowing his head slightly to one and another whom, he imagined, gazed admiringly on so great a hero. No sign did he see of the pickpockets, conscious only of policeman Sansom keeping at a respectful distance behind him.

As he strolled along Goosegate, looking down his haughty nose at two of his sister's friends who had noticed him and were giggling together, he came upon the tea-leaf carrier, shuffling along in front of him. He slackened his pace, not wanting to overtake her, and somehow not feeling very much like a proud duke any more.

In place of the tea-leaves and bread, she was carrying a threadbare woollen blanket, and, with a shock, William realized that she was turning into the shop beneath the sign of three golden balls; the shop which had the words FRANCIS EAMES, PAWNBROKER, written above the door; the shop where William Booth the second was to begin his life's work that very next Monday morning.

Suddenly he remembered the others. Where were they? He'd completely forgotten to tell them about this great change in his affairs. Looking round he saw Will Sansom standing patiently behind him, still at a respectful distance, a quizzical smile on his face.

'Why were you following Besom Jack's wife?' he queried, with a twinkle in his eye. 'Hardly the kind of society for *dukes* to be mixing in!'

'Will, I forgot to tell you,' began the pawnbroker's newest apprentice . . .

'Got you! I've got you!' yelled a voice in his ear. Spinning round, William found Frankie Brown dangling his precious silver pencil-case in front of his eyes. 'If you can't look after your valuables better than that, your Duke-ship, you don't deserve to have them at all!' the pickpocket gloated. 'Now then, ladies and gentlemen, what am I offered for this priceless piece of silver? What in the world am I bid?'

3

WILLIE SHALL HAVE A
NEW MASTER

WILLIAM HATED PAWNBROKING, and that was that.
He had hated it from the moment he'd seen Besom
Jack's wife creeping furtively into 'his' shop to
pawn her rag of a blanket. That was in April; now it
was November and the threadbare blanket still sat
reproachfully on the shelf of unclaimed articles at
the back of the shop, in spite of the frosty nights
when even a threadbare blanket would have spelt
luxury to a thin, bony body.

'But her precious Jack drinks away every bit of
money he can lay his hands on, so she'll never be
able to claim the blanket back again; and I'm no
help. I can't even give her crusts to eat now those
wretched Corn Laws have made bread so ex-
pensive,' grumbled William to 'Cousin Gregory'.
'After all, my six bob a week is hardly enough to
keep Mother and the girls from starving. Oh, how
much I want to do something for the poor!'

He was straddling the workbench of his cousin's
tiny shop, watching another pair of shoes being
fashioned by the long, leathery fingers. How glad he

was of the few precious lunchtime minutes which sometimes allowed him to escape from the penny-pinching pawnshop to the shoemaker's shop close by.

'Mmmm ... I love the smell of leather. It's so clean-smelling after all those fusty, dusty clothes in *our* shop. I hate it! I hate it! I hate it!' muttered William through clenched teeth, hammering his fist on the sturdy workbench and making the tools jump about.

'Now isn't always, Willie,' soothed Cousin Gregory. 'You've your whole life ahead of you. What d'you think you'll do with it?'

'I'll make a fortune and spend it all on the poor,' cried William, his eyes flashing. 'I'll join the Chartists and change the laws of the land so that everyone will have enough and to spare! And little children will never — Do you know, Cousin Gregory, I saw little children crying — for bread — in Kid Street the other day?'

'And do *you* know, Willie Booth, that religion is something inside you that comes to you from outside you?'

'What d'you mean, Cousin Gregory? What's religion got to do with it? There's no religion for the poor. *They* never go to church.'

'But *you* used to, Willie. Do you think you've grown out of such things now you're the head of the house? Do you reckon religion's not for you any more?'

William was silent. Uneasily so. He didn't like the turn the conversation had taken, reminding him of his father's death a few weeks earlier and of the manner of his going. How on earth could a thirteen-year-old find the right words to tell a grown man that he thought his father's death-bed repentance was a last-minute way of getting to heaven?

The church clock never struck a more welcome half hour, and the relieved William vaulted over the workbench, called a hurried goodbye, and was off.

> 'See-saw, Margery Daw,
> Willie shall have a new master;
> He shall have but a penny a day,
> Because he can't work any faster,'

chanted a group of neighbourhood children as William slipped through the side entrance of the pawnshop a few minutes later, hoping Mr. Eames wouldn't notice his arrival.

Trade went briskly for the rest of the day and William had to keep his wits about him. It was Saturday, and many of the poor folk of Nottingham had scraped together enough money to 'redeem' the clothes or bits of jewellery they had left in pledge with the pawnbroker since last Monday. They wanted to wear them on Sunday. William knew that the same articles would be back on the shelves again on Monday for another week; but Mrs. Besom Jack's blanket never had such a Sunday airing.

'See-saw, Margery Daw, Willie shall have a new master.' The words circled round and round in his exhausted head that night as he waited for sleep to come. He had worked from seven-thirty in the morning until turned midnight (as he did most Saturdays), and now the church clock that didn't know how to strike thirteen was striking a dismal one.

'Willie shall have a new master . . .'

'Feargus O'Connor, the Chartist leader? Will *he* be my master?' he wondered.

'Do *you* know, Willie Booth, that religion is something inside you that comes to you from outside you?' Cousin Gregory's words joined the chorus that hammered in his brain. 'Willie shall have, Willie shall have, Willie shall have a new master . . .'

4

THE MAID WAS IN THE GARDEN HANGING OUT THE CLOTHES

'WELL, IF IT isn't the Iron Duke himself,' said a familiar voice in William's ear as he was strolling along Broad Street late one evening in 1844.

'Boldie Newbold!' he laughed, turning in the direction of his old friend, and remembering that last good game of pickpocketing nearly two years before. 'Where d'you think *you're* going, all dressed up like a dog's dinner?'

'I'm going home now,' Boldie answered, 'but I've just been to a Class Meeting at Wesley Chapel.'

'What's that all about then?' William's curiosity was continually getting the better of him, and a Class Meeting was something he hadn't come across before.

'Well, it's a group of Methodists who meet on a weeknight to study the Bible and talk about how they're getting on.' Boldie ran a finger round the inside of his collar, feeling very self-conscious because he was quite certain that young Booth was going to laugh at him for being a softie.

'What d'you mean, "How they're getting on"?'

To Boldie's relief, William wasn't laughing. All the same the young Methodist blushed and stammered his way through his first confession of faith. 'Um . . . well, how they're getting on . . . um . . . at being . . . um . . . Christians.'

'Oh,' said William. Then remembering something his Methodist cousin, Gregory, had said over a year ago, he asked: 'Boldie, do you believe that religion is something inside you that comes to you from outside you?'

'Why, yes, Willie, yes I do! Religion comes to a person from . . . God.' He noticed that his friend was looking thoughtful, and plucking up courage he said: 'Willie, why don't *you* come along to Brother Carey's class next week? You'd enjoy it!'

'Willie shall have a new master . . .' For some unaccountable reason the words flashed through William's head.

He did *not* enjoy Brother Carey's class; it made him feel uncomfortable, particularly when that gentleman asked the young pawnbroker's apprentice how he was 'getting on in his soul'. He knew he really wasn't 'getting on' very well at all, and he felt guilty about it. Yet somehow he couldn't stop going to Wesley Chapel, unhappy though he was.

'I say, missus, if your heart's not washed cleaner than those clothes, you'll never get to heaven!' William heard a man shouting early one morning as his long legs sped him in the direction of the pawnshop to keep his daily appointment with the poor.

'Come and hear how to get a clean heart tonight at Wesley Chapel!'

'That must be the famous Isaac Marsden,' the boy thought to himself, his boots clattering over the cobbles. 'Wonder if I'll finish work in time to hear him?' He did.

With Boldie Newbold and Will Sansom, he entered the chapel in the dusk of the evening. The service had long since started, and the gloom made it difficult for them to see the preacher. But they could hear him!

'A soul dies every minute!' Isaac Marsden was telling a breathless congregation in no uncertain terms.

'If Boldie and Will weren't with me, I'd give myself to God *now*,' William told himself. 'I want to be right with God, I want to be right with myself, and I want a life spent in helping other people to be right.'

Something besides his friends was holding him back. Something was definitely getting in the way of his becoming a Christian. For a long time it worried William that he couldn't put his finger on that something. Then late one night walking in a disconsolate fashion through Nottingham's deserted streets, his struggle ceased. As the church clock struck eleven, William remembered the pencil-case.

'If you don't look after your valuables, your Duke-ship,' Frankie had gloated two years back, 'you don't deserve to have them at all!'

'That's right!' gasped William, clapping his

hands to his ears as though to shut out the remembered voice, 'I don't deserve to have it at all! My precious silver pencil-case — I don't deserve it! I've never deserved it! I didn't deserve it in the first place!'

Standing in the silent street under a solitary gas lamp, he gazed at his most prized possession. 'I must give it back to Frankie and Walley,' he decided. 'They only gave it to me because they thought I'd done them a good turn. But I hadn't. Yes, they must have it back!'

Still he didn't feel entirely free of his conscience.

Kneeling quietly in a room below Broad Street Chapel, a few days later, 'Willie shall have a new master!' danced into his whirling thoughts once more. 'If I *do* go in for God, I'll do it with all my might!' he told the pencil-case. 'No half-measures! It would be easy simply to *give* you back to Frankie and Walley; it'll be much harder to tell them *why*.'

But tell them why, he did, that very day. Immediately all sense of humiliation and guilt vanished from William's heart. Into his soul flooded an immense feeling of relief and boundless joy, such as he had never experienced in his life before. It bubbled through his whole being, so that his pale, thin face shone with the wonder of it all. He felt as though he wanted to embrace the whole world, so great was his love for God.

'I feel, Will, that I could willingly and joyfully travel to the ends of the earth for Jesus Christ, and suffer anything imaginable to help the souls of other men,' he confided to his friend.

'Willie has *found,* Willie has *found,* Willie has *found* his new Master!' he sang to himself as he set off for home.

5

JACK MAKES A CLEAN SWEEP

The second William Booth was ill. He tossed restlessly on his bed, trying to focus on the dancing brightness the sun's reflection in the water bowl made on the ceiling. He remembered how the first William Booth had died 'of consumption' before reaching twenty-five, and wondered if his namesake would die 'of the fever' before reaching eighteen.

While he was occupied with such morbid thoughts his mother brought in a letter with a stamp on it which, even though the Penny Post had been in existence for six years, still created a sense of excitement in such a poverty-stricken home as theirs.

'It's for you, William,' she said.

William opened it carefully and read aloud, '1846. My dear William, I was sorry to know that you had been so sick with the fever and earnestly pray that you are feeling better by now. Since listening to the American preacher, Revd. James Caughey, I have been challenged to do more for my God. I have therefore decided to start holding open-air meetings in the slums of the town and I badly need your help. Hurry up and get better! Your friend, Will Sansom.'

William lay back on his pillows and within an hour the fever had died down. A friend needed his help and he was determined to live long enough to give him that help.

Later that week William was once more alone in the house when the tea-leaf carrier called. He tottered weakly into the scullery, found the teapot and shook the leaves into her thin, grimy hands.

'You live in Kid Street, don't you, mother?' the tall bean-pole-of-a-boy asked her. She nodded her head, gazing at the tea-leaves, ashamed to meet his grave grey eyes.

'I'd like to visit you there sometime,' he said. 'I'd like to meet your Jack. In fact, I'd like to hold a short religious meeting in your house — for you and Jack and the neighbours.'

The woman's eyes met William's in terror. 'Nay, lad, don't do that! 'E'll thrash the livin' daylights outta you.'

She was shaking her life-weary head and would have laid beseeching hands upon his arm, but for the tea-leaves.

'Don't do it, lad!' she repeated. ' 'Sides, none o' them neighbours'll come to my 'ouse — not wi' our Jack about.'

'Never mind, Mother,' he said gently. 'I'll find a way. Don't be fearful now.'

William's mind was busy during the next few days, and as soon as he was well enough to go out he

arranged to meet Will Sansom in Kid Street. No
longer were children crying for bread in that slum.
An Act of Parliament had, that year, brought
down the price. Nevertheless, everywhere there was
misery and squalor and stench.

Will Sansom carried an old wooden chair which
he put down in the gutter outside Besom Jack's
hovel. Standing on it, book in hand, he shouted out
the words of a Methodist hymn:

> Outcasts of men, to you I call,
> Harlots and publicans and thieves!
> He spreads His arms to embrace you all;
> Sinners alone, His grace receives:
> No need of Him the righteous have,
> He came the lost to seek and save.

By the time the two Williams had sung hoarsely
through this hymn they were surrounded by a
noisy, ridiculing crowd. At short intervals, an over-
ripe tomato or other piece of gutter refuse found its
well-aimed way to an obvious part of the preacher's
anatomy. The moment the second William Booth
made his appearance on the chair his 'Wellington's
beak' became an ideal moving target.

'Friends,' he called out, dodging the filthy am-
munition. 'Friends, I want to put a few straight
questions to your souls. Have any of you got a child
at home without shoes to its feet? Are your wives
sitting now in dark houses waiting for you to
return without money?'

Just then Besom Jack lumbered out of his mis-
erable cottage and made straight for William, who

was shouting, 'Are you going away from here to the public-houses to spend on drink, money that your wives need for food and your children for shoes?'

'You leave my missus outta this!' roared Jack, lunging at the preacher. The crowd eased back in cautious delight.

'Jack, God loves your wife, and so did you once,' said William steadily, and the broom-seller immediately gentled down. 'Can you remember how much you loved her and cherished her when first you met?' the boy asked tenderly. Jack nodded, his eyes fixed on the ground.

'Well, Jack, God loves *you* with a love like that, with a love far deeper and greater than that.'

The hushed crowd strained to catch what the boy-preacher was saying, amazed at the change that had overcome the drunkard.

Jack lifted his eyes and blinked sheepishly at William.

'*Me?*' he said in wonderment.

'Yes, Jack, you.' And William, down from the chair by this time, took Jack's arm . . .

'And 'e said to 'im,' "Come, Jack, just kneel down 'ere and tell the Lord you love 'im too",' recounted Jack's wife to Mr. Eames the pawnbroker the following week, ' "And ask 'im ter fergive yer." And 'e did! My Jack knelt there in the gutter and 'e's bin a different man ever since; 'e says 'e's a Christian now!'

Mr. Eames scratched his head and hardly knew what to believe. Jack's wife pushed a handful of coins and a grubby pawn ticket across the counter and Mr. Eames believed her at last.

'I'd like me blanket back now, Mr. Eames; the one I left 'ere four years ago. Remember?'

When William arrived for work the next morning, the shelf at the back of the shop looked strangely bare.

'Well, Jack, you *have* made a clean sweep of it this time,' he smiled softly to himself.

6

THE SHOEMAKER'S HOLIDAY

'LONDON-TOWN, London-town, London-town, London-town,' chuntered the wheels of the railway train, speeding William towards the capital city at such an alarming rate. His pawnbroking apprenticeship had ended a year ago and, as Mr. Eames was not in a position to employ him any longer, William had been searching for work in Nottingham ever since. There was none. His mother and two younger sisters badly needed his support. There was nothing else for it but — 'London-town, London-town, London-town, London-town,' bleak and big and heart-breaking.

Sitting bolt upright in an open-sided third-class carriage, William was completely unaware of this heart-break — he who had so lately asked his friend, Walley James: 'Have you no ambition? Because I have; I intend to be something great.'

Standing outside the firmly locked door of his sister Ann's house, several hours later, he felt quite the opposite of great. The joy of once again being in the company of Ann and her husband, Francis

Brown (the successful pickpocket of his childhood games), was abruptly shattered. An alcoholic husband, having once taught his wife to drink, was hardly likely to welcome the brother-in-law who had preached such characters as Besom Jack away from 'the drink'. In that moment William first began to sense something of the heart-break of London-town.

Yet more heart-breaking was the discovery he quickly made that if he were to fulfil his ambition 'to be something great', he would have to do it through the hated pawnbroking trade. The only employment he could find was with a pawnbroker whose premises at Kennington Common in South-East London also provided an attic bedroom.

'Work, work, work, morning, noon and night,' wrote William, having only Sundays free for the business of preaching about Jesus Christ, the Saviour of men. And then the rule was, home by ten o'clock, or the door would be locked against him. Many a time in the next two years it very nearly was.

Then, for the *second* time in his twenty-two years, William came upon a wise shoemaker. Not in the least like quiet Cousin Gregory was wealthy Edward Rabbits, but a shoemaker none the less, and a Methodist too. In the Walworth Road Wesleyan Chapel, William and Mr. Rabbits first met; William the preacher, and Mr. Rabbits the delighted listener.

'Mr. Booth, you must come home to dinner!' enthused Mr. Rabbits, shaking William's hand vigorously as he left the chapel. 'That was a splendid sermon this morning.'

'Thank you, sir,' said the amazed William. Not often had London-town offered such warmth.

'Why don't you become a minister?' asked Mr. Rabbits as they walked towards the house.

William could not *think* why, and said so. To be a minister, preaching the Good News of Jesus Christ to the world, was all he longed for now.

The shoemaker decided to see what could be done about the idea.

'What did you think of the sermon last Sunday, Miss Mumford?' Mr. Rabbits asked the young woman he met on Clapham Common several weeks later.

'Mr. Booth's, do you mean?' she replied, smilingly. 'I think he preached the best sermon I have ever heard! I must certainly hear him again!'

Two weeks later she did; William was one of the tea-party guests whom she met in Mr. Rabbits' drawing room.

'Tell me about that beautiful-voiced Miss Mumford,' said William to the shoemaker on that occasion. 'I must certainly hear her again!'

The shoemaker decided to see what could be done about *that* idea, too.

Meanwhile, he had been busy thinking about the *first* idea. William must become a minister soon.

'How much can you live on, William?' he queried.

'Um ... well, I don't see how I could get along with less than twelve shillings a week.'

William Booth

'Nonsense!' said Mr. Rabbits. 'You cannot do with less than twenty shillings a week, I am sure.'

William, once more amazed at London-town's warmth, became bolder.

'All right,' he said, 'have it your own way, if you will; but where is the twenty shillings to come from?'

'I will supply it!' declared the shoemaker; and the bargain was struck there and then.

With pawnbroking behind him for ever, William found two rooms for five shillings a week, which he furnished with 'some chairs and a bed', and 'felt quite set up'.

Next day, Good Friday, April 9, 1852, being a holiday, the shoemaker was on his way to a religious meeting in London's East End, when he happened upon the newly-free William, loping along in a similar direction.

'Where are you bound, young Booth?' he enquired.

'To visit a cousin, sir,' said William. Without much effect it would seem, since before he knew what was happening, he found himself accompanying the shoemaker, who had been busy thinking about the *second* idea.

Sure enough, Miss Mumford was at the meeting; and sure enough, she needed company in making the exhausting journey back to Brixton; and sure enough, her mother invited him in; and sure enough, William had found his Catherine; and tomorrow? Tomorrow he would be twenty-three.

7

IF I HAD A DONKEY AND
HE WOULDN'T GO...

TEN YEARS AFTER William had found his Catherine a four-year-old girl stood on tip-toe, gazing into the cradle of her four-week-old brother and whispering: 'Baby Herbert, I'm going to tell you a secret. I'm the *second* Catherine Booth! Mama's the *first*, and I'm the *second*.'

'Mama's the *first* and you're the *second*,' echoed two-year-old Emma who was playing near by, and the second Catherine Booth's secret was out in a moment.

'Mama's the *first* and Katie's the *second*; Mama's the *first* and Katie's the *second*,' chanted Emma to her doll, as she rocked it vigorously in the rocking chair.

Six-year-old Bramwell, chasing five-year-old Ballington into the nursery just at that minute, stopped in his tracks to listen to this latest piece of family gossip.

'Mama's the first and Katie's the second *what*?' he questioned, taking Emma's curly head in his hands. 'Katie's the second *what*, little Emma?'

Reluctant as she was to displease Bramwell, Emma could not for the life of her *think* what; which, after all, isn't surprising, since most two-year-olds haven't much of a memory for facts.

'Katie, Mama's the first and you're the second *what?*' tried Bramwell again that afternoon, in an attempt to get to the bottom of the tantalizing secret.

The children were walking by the sea at Penzance with their mother, as they did most afternoons since their move to Cornwall. Clutching her mother's hand more possessively, and filled with a growing sense of importance, Katie decided that here was a secret too good to keep to herself any longer.

'Mama's the first and I'm the second *Catherine Booth!*' she laughed, glancing up into Mama's lovely face and receiving one of her special 'just for you' smiles.

'When *I* was four years old, Katie, there was *another* Catherine, besides me,' Mama teased.

'How?' asked the wide-eyed little girl.

'Well, I hadn't a big family of brothers and sisters to play with as you have, but I *did* have a family of dolls. I fed them and dressed them and put them to bed and even prayed with them. One of them was called Catherine.'

'Tell us some more, Mama! Tell us some more!' cried Bramwell, trying to tread on his own shadow.

'Goodness me!' the first Catherine laughed. 'Where shall I begin?'

'At the beginning, of course!' chimed in solemn-faced Ballington. 'Every story begins at the beginning.'

'So it does!' said Mama. 'And so did I! I began at a placed called Ashbourne in Derbyshire — up near the middle of England — in 1829, the same year that Papa was born.'

'Had you a mama and a papa?' interrupted Emma, whose memory hadn't improved much since the morning's forgetfulness.

'Of course she had, silly!' laughed Bramwell. 'Who d'you think Grandmama and Grandpapa Mumford are, if they're not Mama's parents? Go on, Mama!'

'Well, by the time I was three, Grandmama tells me, I not only knew my letters, but I could read short words as well.'

'By the time you were *three*?' gasped Bramwell, immediately deciding that at twice that age, he should try to do better with his spelling.

'When I was *your* age, Ballington, I moved with Grandmama and Grandpapa Mumford to Boston in Lincolnshire, where Grandpapa had come from in the first place. There we had a beautiful retriever dog, and wherever I went he would follow me.'

'What was his name, Mama?' Names were very important this afternoon to the second Catherine Booth.

'He was called Waterford and he was the most beautiful creature. One day Waterford had gone with me on a message to my father's house of business. I went in and closed the door, leaving the dog outside, when I happened to strike my foot against something and cried out with the sudden pain. Waterford heard me and, without a moment's hesitation, came crashing through the large glass window to my rescue. My father was so vexed at the damage that had been done, he immediately had the dog shot.'

'Oh, Mama, how terrible! Poor Waterford!' exclaimed Bramwell and Katie together.

'I was dreadfully upset, especially because I realized that it was to rescue *me* that the beautiful creature had lost his life.'

The children were thoughtful for a little while; then they spotted the donkeys.

'Donkeys, Mama!' shouted Emma. 'Look, Mama, donkeys!' and off the children ran in the direction of their patient playmates, leaving the two Catherines to follow at a more sedate pace.

The four rides over, the first Catherine Booth handed an extra sixpence to the donkey boy and said: 'If I were you, I should like to feel, when I went to sleep at night, that I had done my very best for my donkey. I would like to know that I had been kind to it, and had given it the best food I could afford; in fact, that it had had as jolly a day as though I had been the donkey and the donkey me.'

They all laughed at the idea of Mama being a donkey, and as they turned to go, she said to her family: '*That* is how I should like to see my children spend their pennies, in encouraging the boys to be kind to their donkeys. Do you know, children,' she went on, 'one day I was out driving in a carriage with a friend of mine, when I saw a boy with a donkey and cart. I noticed him pick up a stick and hit the donkey with it, but as we drove past I saw that it wasn't a stick but a heavy-headed hammer which had already made a dreadful wound in the poor donkey's back.'

'Oh, Mama!' cried the sensitive Bramwell 'What did you *do* about it?'

'I called the coachman to stop, but before he could do so, I flung myself down into the road (tripping over my dress in the hurry) and rushed to the donkey and seized its reins. That wicked boy tried to drive on; but he couldn't because I was clinging to the shaft. I was extremely angry with him and made him give me the hammer and his name and address.'

'And then, Mama?'

'And then I fainted away!' laughed the first Catherine Booth.

That night as the children lay in bed, William and Catherine could hear them chanting softly:

> If I had a donkey and he wouldn't go,
> Do you think I'd beat him? No, no, no.
> I'd put him in a stable and give him
> lots of corn,
> He'd be the best little donkey that
> ever was born.

8

THE 'CONVERTING' SHOP

As THE CHILDREN grew older, they became more and more fascinated in hearing stories of their parents' earlier years. The conversion of Besom Jack was always a firm favourite, as was the one about what they were later to call 'Mama's first open-air procession'.

Running along the road in Boston one day, bowling a hoop with a stick, young Catherine Mumford had heard a good deal of shouting. In the manner of many a normal nine-year-old, Catherine's curiosity got the better of her and, before she knew it, she found herself at the front of a jeering crowd. Suddenly she realized what all the commotion was about: a prisoner was being dragged to the lock-up by a constable.

'And not one of Will Sansom's sort, either!' explained Papa to the children, reminding them of the pickpocket story.

To Catherine it seemed as though all the world was against the prisoner; his utter loneliness touched her sensitive soul. Quick as lightning she sprang to his side and marched down the street with him, determined that he should feel at least one heart sympathizing with him, whether it was his fault or misfortune that had led him into trouble.

'And she was only nine!' her children would tell each other in admiration, adding with awe: 'And she read the Bible through eight times from cover to cover before she was twelve!' But then Mama, as they were soon to learn, was a very remarkable person.

Best of all, the young Booths liked to hear 'the Rabbits story', for that was all about how their parents had first met. They loved to persuade Mama to show them the part she had written in her diary as a young girl describing the sort of man she would like to marry:

> He must be a sincere Christian; not a nominal one or a mere church member, but truly converted to God. He should be a man of sense — I could never respect a fool, or one much weaker mentally than myself. I will never marry a man who is not a total abstainer, and this from conviction and not merely to gratify me. He should perhaps be a minister. I could be most useful to God as a minister's wife. He should be dark, tall and for preference called William!

'And he was!' the children would chorus when the entry had been read; and they never, in their young hearts, ceased to trace the hand of God in this fairy-tale meeting.

In the listening years of their childhood they

heard with wonder stories of how Mama and Papa went, like gypsies, from town to town in the early days of their marriage. God's gypsies they were, telling every one the good news of His love. They lived in so many different places in such a small handful of years, that Bramwell, Ballington and Katie were all born in different towns. Only at Gateshead, where Papa was in charge of the same Methodist chapel for three years, did Emma manage to catch up with Katie who had also been born there, a year-and-a-half before. By the time Herbert was born, two-and-a-half years later, they had moved on again.

Although Mama had told the children that Papa had hated the pawnbroking shop of his Nottingham days so much that he could never bear to mention it, they often heard him talking about the Gateshead 'shop'. That was a different kind of shop altogether! It was, in fact, a chapel. Such crowds crammed the pews and aisles and stairs to hear Papa preach, and so many people became Christians as a result, that throughout the neighbourhood it came to be known as the 'Converting Shop'. Marvellous things happened at Gateshead ('Besides the births of Katie and Emma!' Papa would laugh).

Papa organized the chapel members into a procession every Sunday evening and paraded the streets from five to six o'clock, singing as they went. Sometimes groups of men were sent out from the public houses to try to bawl loudly enough to drown the Methodists' hymns. Then Papa (who never could resist a good sing) would lead his procession in singing religious words to the same music-hall tune the roughs were using, so defeating them at their own game.

'And there it was that you learnt to "p'each", as you called preaching, when you were only three years old, Bramwell'.

'Now tell us about what happened to *you* Mama!' one of the children would plead.

Then the first Catherine Booth would recount how one Sunday evening she was passing along a street in the poorest area of Gateshead, on her way to hear Papa preach in chapel, when a voice spoke to her:

'Wouldn't you be doing God more service by inviting these poor folk to the chapel than by going to enjoy it yourself?'

Mama, very frightened at the idea, answered, 'Lord, if Thou wilt help me, I will try.'

She talked to one and another of the little groups of women who were standing at the doors and sitting on the doorsteps, and she was just wondering where she should go next, when she saw a woman on a step with a jug in her hand.

'Speak to that woman,' she heard the voice within her say. Immediately a second voice murmured: 'Ah, but perhaps she is drunk!' (The devil was always trying to frighten Mama.) After a struggle within herself, Mama began: 'Are the people out who live on this floor?'

'Yes,' the woman said. 'They've gone to chapel.'

'I'm so glad to hear that,' replied Mama with her lovely smile, 'but how is it that you haven't gone too?'

'Me?' she queried, looking down at her forlorn appearance. 'I can't go to chapel; I'm kept at home by a drunken husband.'

This was Mama's big opportunity to help God. 'May I come and see your husband?' she asked.

'No. He's drunk; you couldn't do anything with him now.'

'I don't mind that, if you will just let me in.' Up the stairs Mama followed the woman and into a small room on the first floor, where a fine, intelligent-looking man of about forty was sitting almost double in a chair, with a jug by his side out of which he had been drinking.

Then Mama would tell the children of how she had begun to talk to the drunken man very gently, all the while listening for what God wanted her to say. So clearly did she tell the story that her family could almost *see* the poor man gradually raising himself in his chair and listening to her with a surprised, half-vacant stare. Then as she read to him the story Jesus had told about the Prodigal Son, the tears ran down his face; 'like rain', remembered Katie from a previous telling.

'And the Lord so helped me in this work that in a few weeks I succeeded in getting ten drunkards to abandon their soul-destroying habits, and to meet me once a week for reading the Bible and for prayer.'

'And the twins, Mama? Tell us about the twins!'

cried Ballington, who knew the story inside out, but always loved to hear it again.

'Oh, those precious twins!' recalled Mama, her eyes growing misty. 'One day I went into a room in a poor part of Gateshead and found a woman lying on nothing but a heap of rags. She had just given birth to twins and there had been nobody at all to help her. By her side was a crust of bread and a small lump of lard — she had no butter. I had to wash the babies in a broken pie-dish because there wasn't a tub.'

' 'Magine that,' said Katie, wide-eyed with pity, as she helped Mama to bath Bertie that evening. 'There wasn't even a tub to wash those babies in!'

'And all because there's wickedness in the world, Katie. Do you know, little one, I would rather my boys grew up to be chimney-sweeps and my girls grew up to be scullery maids, than that they should grow up wicked.'

And there and then the second Catherine Booth decided that whatever else she was to grow into, wicked was the one thing she would not be.

9

WITHOUT A FRIEND
AND WITHOUT A FARTHING

As FAR BACK as her children could remember,
Catherine had been just as busy preaching the good
news of Jesus Christ as William. That was because
the children were young and their memories
younger. 'Now' certainly hadn't been 'always', as
far as Catherine's preaching was concerned. In fact
it wasn't until after Emma's birth, when Catherine
was thirty-one, that God had spoken to her about
this special way of helping Him. 'Another of the
marvellous things that happened at Gateshead,'
William had told the children.

Though ruled by a Queen, Victoria's England
gave women little encouragement to be anything
other than wives and mothers. Certainly not
preachers! Catherine had long been aware of this.
Having read the Bible through eight times before
she was twelve, she had also long been aware that
the biblical view of women was quite different from
the Victorian view. In her Bible she learnt that in
'Christ Jesus there is neither ... male nor female,
but ye are all one in Christ Jesus', and she spent

much thought and many hours (in between caring for her babies and her drunkards) in writing a booklet about it. As far as Catherine was concerned, she had done what she could. As far as God was concerned, she had hardly begun.

Three months after Emma's birth Catherine was sitting one Sunday morning in chapel with four-year-old Bramwell, listening to that part in the service where people tell one another 'how they're getting on at being Christians' (as Boldie Newbold had explained it to William all those years ago in Nottingham).

'Now if you were to speak, you know I would bless it to your own soul, as well as to the people,' she heard the voice within her say.

'Yes, Lord, I believe that, but I cannot do it!' Catherine had answered fearfully.

'Besides,' said the devil, never slow to jump in, 'you are not prepared. You will look like a fool and have nothing to say.' And that was exactly the spur she needed.

'Ah!' she replied, beating the devil with his own stick, 'that's just the point. I have never yet been willing to be a fool for Christ. Now I *will* be one!'

Leaving Bramwell sitting in the pew, Catherine began walking down the aisle towards the pulpit where William was standing. He, thinking that his 'precious Kate', as he called her, must be unwell, rushed down the pulpit steps to meet her.

'What is the matter, my dear?' he asked.

'I want to say a word,' she replied weakly.

William was so taken by surprise that he could

only say to the people, 'My dear wife wishes to speak,' and then he sat down.

'I dare say,' began Catherine shakily, 'I dare say many of you have been looking upon me as a very devoted woman, and one who has been living faithfully to God. But I have been disobeying Him.' Then she went on to tell the great congregation of a thousand people how for a long time God had been asking her to help Him in a special way by preaching the good news of Jesus Christ in chapels and other places, but she had been too afraid.

'Now I have promised the Lord that, from this moment, I will be obedient.'

As Catherine made her way back to the pew where Bramwell was sitting she noticed that many people were so affected by what she had said, that they were weeping.

To her surprise she heard William announcing: 'Tonight, my *wife* will be the preacher.'

Half-an-hour later, Ballington and Katie, too young to have been in chapel, danced round the kitchen table after the maid, who, newly arrived from morning service, was shouting with delight: 'The mistress has spoken! The mistress has spoken!'

That evening the chapel presented a never-to-be-forgotten scene, crowded to the doors, with the people even sitting on the window sills. The audience were spellbound as they listened to Catherine preach, and they continued to be spell-bound when, during the nine weeks William was unable to preach because of illness, Catherine became their minister. As a result, many more people gave themselves to God and became Christians.

While William was ill, an inner voice had been speaking to *him*, too, about the special way he was to help God. So it was that in 1861 the little family left Gateshead 'without a friend and without a farthing', and became God's gypsies once more. In this way they came to Cornwall, where the children made friends with the donkeys, and William and Catherine spent eighteen months preaching the good news of Jesus Christ so effectively that seven thousand men and women were converted to His way of life.

The children remembered their stay in Cardiff, the next port of call, chiefly because of the coming of the *fourth* William Booth (William *Bramwell* was the *third*). The fourth *William Booth* was a ship named after Papa by his new friends, John and Richard Cory. Great was the children's disappointment when they learnt a short time later that it had been wrecked off the island of Bermuda.

Seven-year-old Bramwell had cause to remember Cardiff for another reason. Excited to hear that his parents' services were to be held not in a chapel, but in a circus building, he insisted upon going along with Mama to hear Papa preach.

'Perhaps there will be lions and tigers at the circus!' he said hopefully to Ballington, who wished he could be allowed to go too.

The only lions and tigers at *that* circus were the ones that prowled in Bramwell's own young mind.

After Papa's fiery sermon, while the prayer-meeting was under way and many people were turning to the Lord and making a fresh start in life, Bramwell heard Mama, who was on her knees beside him, saying with great tenderness: 'You are very unhappy?'

'Yes,' he replied.

'You know the reason?'

'Yes.'

Then came the clear question about giving himself to God. Bramwell looked at Mama's beautiful face, so full of eagerness for him to follow Jesus, and then deliberately said: 'No!'

Poor Mama, how unhappy she had felt in the weeks that followed, and how much more unhappy Bramwell felt. So much so, that during their stay at Walsall, Bramwell was amongst the first to kneel at the communion rail in a children's meeting led by Mama.

The child who had begun to 'p'each' at the age of three now took an even greater delight in these make-believe games of preaching. Arranging the nursery as a meeting-place with pulpit and pews, the children 'invited' pillows to the meeting to swell the congregation. Katie and Emma brought their babies, and the babies generally insisted on crying, much to the despair of the preacher (usually Bramwell or Ballington), who stopped preaching to give the stern order, 'Take those babies out of the meeting!' at which the mothers indignantly protested 'Papa wouldn't have stopped! Papa would have gone on preaching!'

There would be hymn-singing and prayers and sermons and collections and a prayer-meeting, always a prayer-meeting. During the prayer-meeting earnest pleas would be made for all sinners there gathered to kneel at the Penitent-form and present themselves to the Lord.

The first to respond to this appeal, almost every time, was one of Emma's most ragged dolls, with her hair all gone, and a great gash in the back of her head — a continual reminder to Bramwell of the day he had had ambitions to become a surgeon. Knife in hand, he had borrowed the doll from Emma, and as the sawdust streamed out of the cut head, Emma's mother-heart wept.

'Silly child!' her brother had exclaimed indignantly. 'Do you think you can have an operation without blood?'

Now it was sick souls, not bodies, that were beginning to claim Bramwell's increasing attention.

10

WILLIAM FINDS HIS DESTINY

'Oh, London is a fine town,
A very famous city,
Where all the streets are paved with gold,
And all the maidens pretty,'

SUNG THE BOOTH children happily as they marched round the garden of the house in Hammersmith, West London, that had lately become their new home. Now there were six of them; baby Marian had joined the family nearly a year before at Leeds.

It was 1865. Mama was busy helping God in the West End of London, while Papa was prowling about the slums of the East End 'looking for work' — God's *particular* work, that only He and Papa knew about. While he was waiting for God's moment to come, Papa spent six weeks preaching every night in a huge tent a group of Christians had set up on an old burial ground in Whitechapel.

One night Papa had arrived home very, very late indeed (Mama had told Bramwell the next day). Mama was sitting by the fire waiting as usual, and as Papa flung himself into the easy-chair opposite her he burst out: 'Oh Kate, as I passed the public houses tonight, I seemed to hear a voice sounding in my ears, "Where can you go and find heathen such as these?" I feel I ought at every cost to stop and preach to these East End multitudes.'

Mama sat gazing into the firelight. She thought of her six children asleep upstairs and of the baby growing within her. She could hear the devil whispering that this would mean yet another start in life, yet another move of house. But she could hear the Lord's voice as well, and she knew it could very well be that God's moment for Papa had come.

'If you feel you ought to stay, stay,' she said quietly. 'We have trusted the Lord *once* for our support, and we can trust Him again!'

Thirteen years earlier William had found his Catherine, now he knew that he had found his destiny.

Almost immediately, he began preaching in the open-air upon a piece of land by the side of the Mile End Road, where shows, shooting ranges, petty dealers and quack doctors rivalled each other in attracting the attention of the poor. The East-Enders regarded the tall, dark preacher as an attraction equal, at any rate, to Punch-and-Judy or the Giant Baby, and as they crowded round him many of them were gripped by the story he told of God's love for them. They followed Papa to the big tent and there discovered the secret of becoming new people in Christ Jesus.

The Booth children thrilled at the stories Papa

Catherine Booth

told them of new converts — like Peter Monk, the Irish prize-fighter — whom God made brave enough to stand in the open-air and tell their old companions 'how they were getting on at being Christians'. Their friends were so impressed by these 'new' men and women, that many of them, too, gave up their old ways of living and began new lives as Christians.

The autumn winds and rains (helped by certain cockney rag-a-muffins) soon demolished the old tent, but the fight against the devil continued in the open-air.

'Papa's original idea was to get the East-Enders converted to God's way and then send them along to the churches and chapels to learn how to be good Christians,' Mama explained to Bramwell. 'But many of the new converts won't go to church, and those that do go, feel so thoroughly out of place that they won't go again.'

'Why do they feel out of place, Mama?' asked her eldest boy, who never felt more 'at home' than when he was in chapel.

'Well, firstly because most of them have never been taught to read, so the church hymn books and prayer books just don't make sense. And secondly, the kind of people who go to church these days aren't anxious to have unwashed, ragged, illiterate folk worshipping alongside them.'

'Papa doesn't mind *who* comes to his services,' said Bramwell, 'as long as people get saved. Where will he hold his meetings now the tent's no use any more, Mama?'

Where indeed?

'The poor are suspicious of going to church or chapel, but they *must* have *somewhere* to worship. What kind of buildings would they go into quite happily?' Papa wondered to himself.

He set about searching for such buildings, asking God to guide him. Bramwell and his brothers and sisters were intrigued by the results of God's guidance: an old dance-hall was found for Sunday meetings, and after the dancing had finished at midnight on Saturdays, Papa organized some of the converts to clear it up, ready for worship on Sundays.

More intriguing still was the building Papa hired for week-night meetings: an old wool warehouse in the roughest part of Bethnal Green. Its windows opened on to the street, and since it was usually packed with people wanting to come to the meetings, the windows were often wide open 'to help drive the smells out and the air in', said Papa sensibly. Even so, the children were always careful not to sit near the windows if ever they went to the meetings, for boys threw stones and mud and fireworks through them, and sometimes these same boys would set fire to trails of gunpowder between the seats — in the middle of Papa's sermons! The Christian Mission members soon got used to these interruptions and would shout 'Hallelujah!' when the crackers exploded and the powder flashed but, to tell the truth, Katie and Emma jumped just as much at the loud 'Hallelujahs' as they did at the fireworks.

As the Christian Mission gained more and more converts, it was necessary to find more and more meeting places. Most of them were every bit as intriguing to the Booth children as the dance hall and the wool shed had been. In Poplar they used a shed between a stable and pigsties, where 'the stench which oozed through the open cracks was enough to have poisoned us all', Papa remembered afterwards. In Old Ford a carpenter's shop was used; in Whitechapel a covered skittle alley 'where they bowled and gambled and drank on week-days, while we preached and prayed and sang on Sunday'. In Shoreditch many people found Jesus in a room twenty feet square in a yard at the back of a pigeon shop.

The children remembered Papa coming home one evening and telling them that the Christian Missioners had been turned out of a stable off Whitechapel Road where, only a week before, they had made a platform and whitewashed the walls.

'Who would do a thing like that, Papa?' asked the second Catherine Booth.

'Our singing disturbed the boxers in the gymnasium next door!' laughed Papa.

So that he could be nearer his 'work', as Mama had feared, the family moved house yet again. This time it was to Hackney in East London. There, on Christmas Day 1865, Mama's special 'Christmas Box' was delivered — a baby girl called Evelyn ('but we'll call her Eva, for short,' the children decided).

'Sit still, Papa, do!' demanded six-year-old

Emma, tugging at William's long mane one evening. Just as Bramwell had had ambitions to become a surgeon, trying out his skill on Emma's doll, so now Emma seemed all set to become a hairdresser, practising her art on Papa's lovely thick hair. It took her a long time to work her way over his whole head with the curl papers, but when she had finally finished she was very well pleased with the result.

At that moment a servant came into the room: 'If you please, sir, there's a visitor to see you.'

Up he sprang, and was almost into the hall when the children flung themselves upon his coat-tails and dragged him back, screaming with laughter. Only then did he look in the mirror over the fireplace and understand why.

'Excuse me, do!' he laughingly explained to the dignified visitor, 'but the Booths are a queer lot!'

'A *very* queer lot!' echoed the children.

11

A QUEER LOT!

ONE MORNING IN the middle of breakfast a year later, Papa, who had been busily opening the day's post, suddenly dropped to his knees in prayer beside the table. Quickly Mama and the children joined him, knowing that something very special must have come in a letter. Then Papa gave thanks to God for the news that some gentlemen, who had heard Mama speak at St. John's Wood, were so impressed with her description of the work of the Christian Mission amongst the poor, that they were promising to give a weekly amount of money towards its work.

No sooner had Papa finished thanking God than up he jumped, burst out laughing and chanted with the children: 'The Booths *are* a queer lot!' It was a catch-phrase they were coming to use more and more about themselves in these exciting days.

'What will you use the money for, Papa?' Ballington asked.

'We'll rent the Effingham Theatre!' cried William, hugging Bertie, who was now nearly five years old.

'The Effingham Theatre?' chorused the children. 'Tell us, Papa!'

'Well, it's a very run-down music-hall in White-chapel Road, and it's packed every night with just the kind of people we want to reach for Jesus.'

'Poor people, Papa?' asked tender-hearted Emma.

'Yes, little Emma, poor people, hopeless people, forgotten people — *God's* people, Emma!'

'They're *God's* people,' remembered Emma when, a few weeks later, she was allowed to go along to a meeting at the Effingham Theatre with Katie and Ballington and Bramwell. If she hadn't kept repeating to herself that they were '*God's* people', Emma would have been very frightened of some of the crowd that packed the theatre from floor to ceiling.

'They're very rough, aren't they, Katie?' she whispered to her sister. 'But Papa says they're *God's* people.'

At a quarter-to-seven the children, sitting in their box, heard the sound of singing as the procession of Christian Missioners marched in from their open-air meeting in Whitechapel Road. Then precisely at seven, they saw Papa make his appearance in front of the footlights on the stage, and give out the hymn:

'There is a better world, they say,
Oh so bright . . .'

The four children joined happily in the singing, and Emma, being only seven and not always able to read all the long words, was particularly glad that such lines as 'Oh so bright' were repeated several times. Many of the East-Enders, not being able to read at all, were equally glad. Everybody seemed to be singing, glorying in it. Bramwell noticed that even hard-featured men and women, in their working clothes and tattered shawls (no 'Sunday best' for them), were standing up amid all the dingy, tawdry, tinselled surroundings of the theatre, to sing of the better world pictured as having 'angels with bright wings' and 'harps of gold' and 'mansions fair'.

In the middle of giving out one verse Papa cried out to one of the Christian Missioners, 'Shut that door!' — which made Ballington giggle.

In the course of another verse Papa came to a dead stop and looked up into a side gallery, combing his hair back with his long fingers. The children, feeling uncomfortable, turned their eyes in the direction in which Papa was gazing. Everybody else looked too, and the men who had been misbehaving themselves suddenly became very quiet.

'Without Papa having to say one word,' Bramwell told Mama much later that night.

Many people had come to the theatre because they had seen posters advertising that the Revd. William Booth was going to tell the ballad of the Blind Beggar. The Christian Missioners sometimes held their open-air meetings outside the Blind Beggar public house in Whitechapel Road, and the Booth children had often heard the story of the beggar of Bethnal Green, who was quite blind, but whose daughter was so beautiful that a king had married her.

Somehow Papa managed to tell the old story in such a way on this occasion that the men and women who had come to hear about the Blind Beggar of Bethnal Green found themselves saying inside themselves: '*I'm* the blind beggar he's been talking about! Blind to the love of God I've been.'

When Papa had finished speaking the children joined the great crowd in singing one of their favourite hymns and prayed in their hearts that lots of sinners would be saved that night, for that would make Papa happy. They sang:

> 'Just as I am, without one plea,
> But that Thy blood was shed for me,
> And that Thou bid'st me come to Thee,
> O Lamb of God, I come!'

And come they did, many of the people, to the front of the theatre where they knelt in prayer to gain strength to begin a new life in the name and in the power of Jesus; and Papa was happy with a deep happiness which made the folk who didn't understand agree that 'the Booths are a queer lot!'

As Christmas 1867 drew near, William said to Catherine: 'Let's give the children a thoroughly happy, old-fashioned Christmas this year, Kate!'

So for a week beforehand the children got more and more excited as every kind of wonderful preparation was made. Then came Christmas morning. From eleven-year-old Bramwell down to two-year-old Eva, the seven children could hardly contain themselves.

William returned from his preaching in Whitechapel, pale, haggard and morose.

'Papa, are you ill?' asked Katie anxiously.

No, he was not ill, and he did his best to enter into the children's fun. Yet it was of no use. He grew more and more gloomy and silent, forgetting the games.

Suddenly he burst out: 'I'll never have a Christmas Day like this again!'

Springing to his feet and walking up and down the room like a caged lion, he told of the sights he had seen that morning in Whitechapel.

'The poor, Emma! The poor have nothing but the public house — nothing but the public house!'

William was true to his word. That Christmas Day was the last the Booth family ever spent in such a way together. The following year, out among the poor, they were giving away plum-puddings (many of them made in Mama's kitchen) and enjoying every moment of being generally thought of as 'a queer lot'.

12

THE WORLD IS WAITING
FOR YOU

ONE DAY IN April, 1868, Papa said to the children:
'Now, listen; I've got a wonderful piece of news for
you. God has sent us a most beautiful present.'

At once there was a shout of 'Is it alive?'

'Yes,' said Papa, 'it's alive.'

'Is it a dog?' cried Katie.

'No.'

'A donkey?' asked Ballington.

'No.'

After a few more guesses at livestock, Papa said,
with great impressiveness: 'It's a baby!'

There was another shout of joy from the children, an instant demand to see the newcomer,
and a creeping upstairs on tiptoe after Papa, to be
shown baby Lucy. Then Ballington, who for some
weeks had been praying industriously for a donkey,
said, *That's* what I've been praying for — a baby!'
and everyone was happy.

William and Catherine's family was now com-
plete.

When Katie was a little girl in socks, Mama

would sometimes say to her: 'Now, Katie, you are not here in this world for yourself. You have been sent for others. The world is waiting for you.' So it was that not only Katie but each of the Booth children grew up wanting above all things to be useful to God in His world.

Yet because they were normal, natural children, things did not always work out quite according to the desires of their highest moments. There was the day Ballington horrified the family by coming home with a shilling ring on his finger — a form of worldliness which dumbfounded Mama and Papa. Emma, the most recent member of the family to have given herself to the Lord, gasped in despair, 'Ballington's a backslider!' a cry which, less kindly, her brothers and sisters quickly took up. 'Ballington's a backslider! Ballington's a backslider!' they chanted.

'Silence!' thundered Papa. 'His mother will deal with him later!'

Tea was eaten in a paralysing silence, while fear filled the mind of the sinner, who scarcely knew whether to be more afraid of God than of his parents.

At the end of the meal Ballington was led by Mama into another room where he remained for ten dreadful minutes, after which he returned to the sitting-room with red eyes, and without the ring!

Soon after this, Bramwell, perched on the scrubbed, white-wood kitchen table, was reading aloud from *The Revival* newspaper while

Mama was doing the ironing, when he came upon a report entitled 'An afternoon with William Booth'.

' "On the afternoon of Sunday, January 31," ' he read, ' "I was able to see some of the results of William Booth's work in the East of London, by attending his experience meeting, held in the East London Theatre. About two o'clock some of his helpers and converts went out together, and held an open-air meeting in front of a large brewery opposite the hall. The ground was damp and the wind high." And the smell from the brewery must have been terrible!' commented Bramwell.

' "But they secured an audience, and then sang hymns along the road till they came to the theatre, taking in any who chose to follow them." ' Bramwell also read to Mama a description of the meeting which lasted one hour and a half, while forty-three people told 'how they were getting on at being Christians', verses of eight hymns were sung, and prayer was offered by four people.

'Does it say anything about Ballington?' Mama asked. 'I think that was the Sunday after the ring episode.'

Bramwell scanned the lengthy report until the name 'Booth' jumped out of the paper at him.

'Here it is, Mama! "A little boy, one of Mr. Booth's sons, gave a simple and good testimony. He was followed by a young man ... and then an interesting blind girl, whom I had noticed singing heartily in the street, told of her conversion last August." '

'Read the bit about Ballington again, Bramwell!'
Mama said.

' "A little boy, one of Mr. Booth's sons, gave a
simple and good testimony," ' read Bramwell, and
Catherine felt quite certain that the ten minutes she
had spent with Ballington on the afternoon of his
backsliding had been very well worthwhile.

Although it was not mentioned in any newspaper
report, Bramwell had his own reason for remembering that particular Sunday. Walking back late
at night through the streets of Whitechapel, Papa
had taken him by the hand and, pushing open a
public house door, pressed into the bar. Bramwell
felt scared; the place was crowded with men, many
of them bearing on their faces the marks of brutish-
ness and vice; there were women as well,
dishevelled and drunken, some with tiny children in
their arms. There, in that brilliantly lighted place,
reeking with fumes of drink, tobacco and filth,
Papa met Bramwell's inquiring gaze by saying:
'These are *our* people; these are the people I want
you to live for and bring to Christ.'

Bramwell never forgot that moment. He began
to look through Papa's eyes at '*our* people'. He
was only twelve when he led his first children's
meeting in a small room at Bethnal Green. In the
middle of his 'sermon' a large rat stood in the door-
way behind the audience, and coolly surveyed the
scene.

'If the children catch a sight of it, there'll be
uproar!' thought Bramwell to himself, so he went
on steadily with his sermon, waving his hands with

all his might in the hope of frightening the visitor
away.

The rat held its ground without flinching. Bramwell spoke more and more vigorously in his at-
tempts to dislodge the enemy, until at length even
the nerves of the East End rat could bear it no
longer. Beating a welcome retreat, the rat left the
speaker to get on with his preaching in peace.

Not so peaceful, however, was the kind of treat-
ment Bramwell received at the City of London
School, after he had won a scholarship. Nick-
naming him 'Saint Booth', the other boys in his
form caught him by the hands and legs and bashed
him against a tree to 'bang salvation out of him',
because he refused to join in any lying and cheat-
ing. Education at home became the pattern for the
Booth children for the most part after that; not for
very long at all did any of them attend school.

'The world is waiting for you.' Mama had told
Katie, and on her twelfth birthday the second
Catherine Booth asked Mama's permission to begin
her work for the world by holding a weekly chil-
dren's meeting in a downstairs room of their Gore
Road house, 'with Emma's help'.

A year later Bramwell was leading an open-air
meeting opposite the Cat and Mutton public house
in Hackney, when Katie, standing beside him,
whispered: 'I will say a few words.'

And so she did, with such effect that many of the
men lounging outside the Cat and Mutton found
themselves listening with growing interest to the
good news of Jesus Christ.

Mama was a little taken aback when she heard about it. For Ballington to have told 'how he was getting on at being a Christian' in an experience meeting in the Effingham Theatre was one thing; quite another for gentle Katie to be raising her voice outside a sleazy East End public house.

'Mama, dear!' said Bramwell tenderly. 'You will have to settle this question with God; for Katie is as surely called and inspired by Him for this particular work as you are yourself.'

And settle it with God Mama did. After all, had it not been she who had always taught Katie: 'You are not here in this world for yourself. You have been sent for others. The world is waiting for you'?

13

THE GENERAL FINDS HIS STAFF

In 1871 seven-year-old Marian caught the dreaded smallpox. It left her disfigured and with permanently injured sight. One of the Booth family was always ill with something. Mixing continually in large crowds of the very poorest people, they invariably fell victim to any epidemic that happened to be going around. Smallpox, scarlet fever, rheumatic fever, measles, whooping-cough, almost every imaginable illness would demand an entrance at their door, and because the family knew that they were not in the world for themselves, but for others, they would never, at any cost, shut that door.

A year later William was so very ill that for six months the doctors feared he would never again be able to work. But William's work (which was *God's* work) could not be that easily put down, and, at sixteen-years-old, Bramwell stepped into the family tradition of shopkeeping. To the experience of the Nottingham pawnshop and the Gateshead converting shop was now added a small chain of four or five Food-for-the-Million shops, which formed yet another part of the Christian Mission's concern for the East-Enders. Bramwell was the manager of these chain-store soup shops providing the poor with 'Hot Soup Day or Night, Three-Course Dinners for 6d'.

With Catherine running the ever-expanding Mission (now spreading like wildfire through East London and on to Croydon, Hastings, Bromley, Tunbridge Wells and beyond), and Bramwell taking on more and more of the business side of things, William was able to spend the last months of his recovery in writing the exciting story of the Christian Mission. One day he was discussing that story with a Methodist minister who said: 'I have a brother who, I think, would just suit you. I must tell him about you.'

'What's that, Papa?' asked Bramwell on William's return to London some time later. William was holding a maroon-coloured pamphlet which he passed to the boy.

'*How to Reach the Masses with the Gospel,*' read Bramwell, 'By William Booth. Price 6d.' Soon he was engrossed in the vivid descriptions Papa had written of the first few years of the Christian Mission's work. Of all the children Ballington was the most proud, for there, on page twenty-three, was the report taken from *The Revival* newspaper which said, 'A little boy, one of Mr. Booth's sons, gave a simple and good testimony.'

The Methodist minister's brother, who, the minister had thought, 'would just suit' William, also heard about *How to Reach the Masses with the*

Gospel and immediately bought a copy. He, too, read about Ballington's testimony. He also read that the Christian Mission's methods 'will be found to be mostly as old as the Acts of the Apostles. Amongst them first and foremost stands the preaching of the Gospel.'

George Scott Railton, liked that. His soul thrilled within him as he read on: 'This kind of work brings with it the result of which the Master spoke. It insures opposition and persecution; it rouses the hatred of men and devils.'

On and on he read, fascinated by William's accounts of the Christian Mission's war against evil and misery and sin. Reaching the end of the pamphlet he finally read: 'We invite our friends to COME AND SEE FOR THEMSELVES. At any date, if they will write to us beforehand, we will arrange for someone to accompany them to any of our stations, or introduce them to any of the persons referred to in this report.'

George Scott Railton wanted to visit *all* the Mission stations; he wanted to be introduced to as many of 'the persons referred to in this report' as possible, but especially to the little boy, one of Mr. Booth's sons, who had given 'a simple and good testimony'. Above all, he wanted to meet William himself. So he wrote to 'Mr. Booth', asking for an appointment to visit him. More than that, he offered his services as a helper in the Mission.

To such extravagant enthusiasm William cautiously replied, inviting Railton to be a guest in the

Booth household for a few days, a prospect which greatly excited the children.

'Papa says that four years ago, when Mr. Railton was nineteen, he journeyed to Morocco to win the Moors for Christ,' Ballington told the others.

'Yes, and he tramped all alone through Morocco and Tunis with a banner which had REPEN-TANCE – FAITH – HOLINESS written on it!' joined in Bramwell. 'And then he ran out of money' ('He only had twenty pounds to start with!' reminded Ballington) 'and had to work his passage home again as a ship's steward.'

If the children were excited by Railton's arrival, Railton himself was excited beyond measure by what he saw of the Christian Mission in London. Instead of a few days, he stayed for weeks with the Booth family and thoroughly endeared himself to their hearts.

One morning they found him fast asleep on top of the scullery copper. He had been out late at a meeting the night before, and, supposing him to have a door-key, the family had gone to bed before his arrival home. Finding himself locked out, and unwilling to disturb the sleeping household, Railton crept in through the coal-hole and curled up on the best substitute for a bed he could find. The Booths might be a 'queer lot', but they quickly discovered that they had met their match in Railton.

To his Methodist minister brother, Railton wrote of his visit to the Booths:

'I have been there and still would go;

'Tis like a little heaven below!'

To William, in January 1873, he wrote: 'My dear General . . . Everything I read about you and your people reawakens and refreshes my love for you all . . . I shall arrive at the right moment and all is well for ever! Your ever-to-be faithful Lieutenant, G.S.R.'

'The right moment' for his arrival came in March of that year and, together with Bramwell, from that time forward he devoted himself to God and to William for the work of the Mission.

As for 'The General', as Railton insisted on calling William, he had at last found his staff.

14

A SORT OF HUNT

DRUNKEN BILL OF Bethnal Green, straggling along with some of his equally drunken friends, elbowed his way into a Christian Mission funeral procession, shouting abuse and menaces at the Booth family in particular and the Mission in general.

'I must do something about him!' Ballington decided to himself.

Remembering the much-loved story of how, as a boy of seventeen, Papa had set about the task of saving Besom Jack in Nottingham, Ballington, now sixteen, resolved to pray and plan for Drunken Bill's conversion with equal determination. Following Papa's example, he first sought out 'Mrs. Bill'.

'I'd like to visit your Bill at home this week,' he told her. 'When's the best time to call?'

'Bless you, lad, our Bill's not wanting any of your religion pushed in 'is face.'

'Never mind that, mother,' persisted Ballington. 'When shall I come?'

'Well, 'e's there now, if you really *want* to come, lad.'

Ballington jumped at the chance, and before Little Bill knew what was happening, he found himself on his knees in his own front room, 'givin' meself to the Lord'.

By the time Emma was sixteen she, too, wanted to be more useful to God. At thirteen, with the help of eight-year-old Eva, she had carried on the tradition, started by Katie, of holding children's meetings in the schoolroom of their home. As she grew older she felt she should do something for 'the poor', who (she remembered Papa saying on that last Christmas Day they had spent as a family) had 'nothing but the public house — nothing but the public house'.

Writing about it for her own children many years later, Emma recorded: 'I remember a particular occasion when God helped me, as perhaps never before. One day, on my way to the little Hackney Mission Hall, I met a rough-looking man. He was standing up against a stone wall, and I was walking to the meeting with somebody, whom I left because I thought I should have a better chance of getting the man to come. Something in my soul made me realize that his need was very great indeed. Stepping across the road, I spoke to him, and at last succeeded in getting him to come with me to the hall. That night that man was saved.

'I found afterwards that he had been away from home for years ... I asked him if he would like me to go home with him ... I shall never forget the impression that little mother's face made upon my heart. She was very short, and her face was wan. As she lifted her arms to get them round this lost boy's neck, I thought she never would have succeeded, for he was a very big man indeed ... As she talked to him, some of the sentences seemed written upon my heart never to be effaced: "With every blessing I have asked at my breakfast I have prayed for you," she said. "And every time I have been out in the open air I have looked for you! Indeed, all my life, Ben, has been *a sort of a hunt* after you!"'

Emma, walking home that night through the darkness, whispered to her Saviour: 'Lord, let that be so with me whatever I have and am, let that be my experience ... that my whole life may be *a sort of hunt* after those whom Thou didst die to redeem ...'

'My dear Eva,' wrote Mama in November, 1876, to her special 'Christmas Box'. 'You have got one of the prettiest names in the English language. I hope your character will match it, because I dislike bad matches in anything, but most of all in names and characters! ... I want you to help Papa in the Mission, if you only grow *good* enough. I want you to help the weak and the poor and the ignorant and the wicked, and lead them to Jesus and to heaven ...'

So it was that yet another of Catherine's children received her marching orders, young though she was.

To Bramwell, the following year, Mama wrote: 'I believe it was the Lord who led us to *begin* the work, and it seems to me He has "grown" you up on purpose to carry it on, for certainly no one else

could have given you *such a heart for it* but
He . . .'

To folk who remarked that that queer lot, the
Booths, 'put their children into the Movement too!'
Catherine would reply: 'Yes, bless God! and if we
had twenty, we would do so. But . . . it is all from
the same motive and for the same end, *the seeking
and saving the lost.*'

'The world is waiting for you,' said Mama to
Katie.

'These are *our* people . . . the people I want you
to live for and bring to Christ,' said Papa to Bramwell.

'Lord, that my whole life may be *a sort of hunt*
after those whom Thou didst die to redeem,' said
Emma to the Lord.

And what a glorious sort of life it was all proving
to be!

15

ARMY OF SALVATION

'BUT WHERE WILL you get your preachers, Mr. Booth?' asked a Christian Missioner one day, when the General Superintendent was declaring his intention to open still more Mission stations.

'Out of the public houses,' was the prompt reply William gave, and, in fact, some (though not by any means all) of his best preachers were men and women who had discovered in Jesus Christ a far greater source of satisfaction and joy than they had ever found in the drink to which they had once devoted their lives. Typical of them was Elijah Cadman, God's chimney-sweep.

'Small boys for narrow flues' was a common advertisement put out by chimney sweeps in the mid-nineteenth century, and six-year-old Elijah Cadman, the last of a family of five and unusually small, was ideally suited to such an occupation.

Beginning his day's work at four in the morning whatever the weather, he continued to climb up and down chimneys until he was thirteen, when a law was passed preventing boys being used in that way. From the age of six he was often drunk, and by the time he was seventeen he could 'fight like a devil and drink like a fish'.

One Christmas Day he was watching a public execution by hanging at Warwick, when someone said, pointing to the dangling bodies: 'That's what you'll come to, 'Lijah, one day!'

So shocked was he at the thought that he immediately gave up drinking and made sure that a few other folk gave up too; going through the villages and ringing a town crier's bell in front of each inn until a crowd gathered.

'This is to give notice, 60,000 people are lost,' he would bawl. 'Lost! Lost! Lost! Lost every year through the cursed drink. Mr. Cadman, the Sober Sweep from Rugby, will give an account of his own drinking experiences! Come and hear him! Come and hear him!'

But not until he was twenty-one did Elijah become a Christian — as a result of listening to a street-preacher with whom he had intended starting a row. Soon Methodist lay-preaching filled every spare moment left over from his chimneys, and he decided to teach himself to read by taking on a class of forty or fifty infants for reading lessons. Holding up an old-fashioned alphabet board, he pointed to a letter.

'What's that?' he asked the children.

Silence. Then a shrill cry: 'The board's upside down!'

'So it is,' said Elijah who, in his ignorance, knew not one end of a letter from the other. Turning the board the other way up, again he asked: 'What's that?'

'A,' said a child.

'Is he right?' thought Elijah to himself and, to make sure, he asked every child the name of the letter, as a means of getting it into his own head. After three weeks he knew the name and shape of all twenty-six letters and a number of short words as well, but his teaching methods were less than conventional.

'What's that?' he asked the children, pointing to the word 'At', and when none of them appeared to know the answer, he decided to give them a clue. 'What d'you wear on your 'eads?' he beamed. 'An 'at! That's right, you've guessed it! The word's "at"!'

When Elijah was twenty-two 'the Lord told me I was to get married!' he often recounted afterwards.

'Yes, Lord. When?' he had answered.

'Next Christmas,' was the instruction.

'Yes, Lord,' said Elijah. But when, the following September, the Lord reminded him again that he was to be married by Christmas, he replied, 'Lord, how can that be? I haven't got a girl.'

Not long after, he was sweeping the chimneys belonging to a master of Rugby School, when he met the pretty parlour maid of the house. 'And it came to me that it was *Her*!'

What should he do next? he wondered, and was advised to send a letter asking her to marry him. No answer did he receive, and so it was not until some time later, when he went to sweep those same chimneys again, that he met his pretty parlour maid once more.

'Good morning!' he said.

'Good morning!' she returned.

'Did you get a letter from me?'

'Yes.'

'What did you think of it?'

'Nothing at all!'

'Well,' said Elijah, throwing all the entreaty he possibly could into his voice and eyes, 'let me know "yes" or "no" by tomorrow morning's post, because I can't stand any longer waiting.'

Next day Maria's letter came. It said 'yes', and at Christmas 1865 (much the same time as Catherine's special 'Christmas Box' was arriving) Maria and Elijah were joyfully married.

"Lijah, I've seen a people in London who live to serve Christ, and they're our class!' said a friend one day in 1876. So off Elijah went to see the Christian Mission for himself.

'Eva, look!' whispered Lucy Booth, now aged eight, nudging her sister as they sat waiting one Sunday for the evening meeting to begin in the Mission's Whitechapel Hall. A prosperous tradesman now, owning his own shop as well as a partnership in the chimney-sweeping business, Elijah Cadman, dressed in a well-cut suit and wearing a tall silk hat, instantly claimed the attention of the children, in spite of his shortness.

By that summer, Elijah had sold his house and business and moved with his wife and children to take charge of the Christian Mission station at Hackney in East London, where, among other things, he 'rescued various intending suicides from their purpose and saw an organ grinder and potato man converted. In previous opposition the one had sought to drown the speakers at an open-air meeting with his music, while the other had bombarded them with hot potatoes!'

In October 1876 he reported to William: 'We are making a powerful attack upon the devil's kingdom ... King Jesus is our great Commander ... We have an Army here that will face the world, the flesh and the devil.'

A year later William sent Cadman to 'open fire' on Whitby. More and more the Missioners were adopting military-sounding phrases and methods in their fight against the devil, and the man-in-the-street, expecting England to go to war at any moment against Russia, was instantly attracted by it all. Announcing his arrival in Whitby, Cadman had a poster made which read:

WAR! WAR! IN WHITBY

2,000
MEN AND WOMEN
Wanted at once to join the
Hallelujah Army

(contd. over)

That is making an attack on the
devil's kingdom

every Sunday in
ST. HILDA'S HALL at 11 a.m., 3 and
6:30 p.m.

To be led by CAPTAIN CADMAN from

London

Evangelist of The Christian Mission

As a result three thousand people regularly attended his meetings.

Cadman had been in Whitby four weeks when William decided to visit this newest of Mission stations. His arrival was heralded with another 'War' poster:

MR. BOOTH THE GENERAL
of the
HALLELUJAH ARMY

is coming to

WHITBY

TO REVIEW THE TROOPS

GREAT BATTLES
WILL BE FOUGHT

At the beginning of May 1878 'the General' summoned his 'staff' to his bedroom early one morning to discuss the day's business with them. Dressed in a long yellow dressing-gown and slippers, William paced up and down the room, while Railton and Bramwell sat at a table strewn with papers, ready to write at his bidding. They were working upon an article for the Christian Mission report, and Railton began reading aloud what he had so far written: 'The Christian Mission, under the superintendence of the Rev. William Booth, is a VOLUNTEER ARMY recruited from amongst the multitudes who are without hope in this world—'

'Here,' interrupted Bramwell. 'I'm not a volunteer; I'm a regular or nothing!'

William stopped in his tracks, gazed at Bramwell hard, then leaning over Railton's shoulder, took the quill pen from his hand, scratched out the word 'VOLUNTEER' and wrote over the top of it 'SALVATION'.

Railton began reading again: 'The Christian Mission, under the superintendence of the Rev. William Booth is a *SALVATION* ARMY . . .'

In that early morning moment, thirteen years after the beginning of the Christian Mission, The Salvation Army found its name.

16

THE DEVIL'S THE THIEF

THE BOOTHS WERE a song-writing family. Herbert, the musician of the family, was always composing new tunes or setting new words to old music hall tunes. William, Bramwell, Ballington, Katie, Emma, Eva and Lucy were also often busy in verse-writing, and many of their deeply religious songs are used in Salvation Army meetings to this day.

Long before he and Catherine were married, William wrote to her that he had been turning over a heap of music at the booksellers that morning to find tunes that his precious Kate could fit to religious words. A piece of music called the *Bridal Waltz* he thought might be adapted to religious words, but alas, its price was four shillings! 'Shall I buy it?' he asked of Catherine, 'I have no notion of giving so much for *the devil's music*, but your will shall be done.'

Much later, when the Christian Mission was rapidly developing into The Salvation Army, it became William's habit to adopt rousing, lively tunes (very often played by brass bands) to attract folk to his meetings. When 'respectable' people complained about this, he used Whitefield's reply when, a hundred years earlier, that nonconformist had been accused of singing hymns to ungodly, but gay, tunes: 'Very true, sir; very true. But pray, sir, can you assign a good reason why the devil should always have the best tunes?'

George Scott Railton was quick to seize upon this method of song-writing. Salvationists the world over still sing words Railton wrote to such tunes as 'A life on the ocean wave' and 'Marching through Georgia'.

'Not allowed to sing that tune or *this* tune? Indeed!' wrote William in the Christmas edition of the Army's paper *The War Cry* in 1880. 'Secular music, do you say? Belongs to the devil, does it? ... Well, ... he's the thief! ... Every note and every harmony is divine and belongs to us ...'

Here are two typical 'fun' songs which early-day converts used to sing. The first is a Christian Mission song:

> Oh! the Christian Mission is a grand device,
>   Glory Hallelujah.
> For turning this earth into paradise,
>   Sing glory Hallelujah.
>
> Chorus:— Hallelujah, Glory Hallelujah!
>   Hallelujah, Glory Hallelujah!
>   Hallelujah to the Lamb,
>   Sing, Glory Hallelujah.

They said it was only a flash in the pan,
But the flash a glorious fire began.

In the streets, in the lanes, aye, anywhere,
Our cathedral is the open-air.

We may be rough and speak aloud,
But our words are blessed to the hardened
  crowd.

Yes, saving souls is our delight,
Whether 'tis morning, noon or night.

We're soldiers fighting for our God,
And we shall conquer through the blood.

And of all we've seen, or hope to see,
We give the glory, Lord, to Thee!

The second song is a kind of Salvation Army
ballad — a song which tells a story:

One day I was passing along a back street,
When a band of small children I chanced
  to meet;
And thus they were singing together at play,
"Salvation forever, Salvation, hurray!"

"We once lived on dry bread and what we
  could get,
And when we had nothing, we hardly dared
  fret;
But now we have bread and nice treacle
  each day,
Salvation forever, Salvation, hurray!'

"Our houses were empty, we scarce had
   a chair,
And strong drink had broken our
   crockery-ware;
"We've now chairs and tables,
   and china so gay,
Salvation forever, Salvation, hurray!

"Our fathers were such, they had learnt to
   drink ale,
Our mothers were ragged, their faces were
   pale;
But Salvation breezes blew rags right away,
Salvation forever, Salvation, hurray!"

And finally, here is a chorus that early-day Salvationists sang to the tune of 'That Daring Young Man on the Flying Trapeze':

I'm a Salvation soldier from top to toe,
I fight the old devil wherever I go,
I live for King Jesus, my colours to show;
I belong to The Salvation Army!

17

AN 'APORTH OF 'APPY 'LIZAS

'I WOULD LIKE to wear a suit of clothes that would let everyone know I meant war to the teeth and salvation for the world!' declared God's chimney-sweep, Elijah Cadman, in the same year the Christian Mission first became known as The Salvation Army.

'If an Army, why not a uniform?' agreed Catherine, whereupon Cadman and Railton at once set about making crude, home-made badges to wear on their hats.

Intrigued by the idea, Herbert, now sixteen, arrived at the Bethnal Green Meeting Hall wearing a helmet he had made himself, with a Salvation Army crest worked on the front. The girls immediately labelled him the 'Salvationist bobbie' (the Peelers of William's boyhood now being more widely known by Sir Robert Peel's other nickname).

Before September was out, the first Salvation Army flag had been presented by Catherine to Captain Mrs. Caroline Reynolds, who had started the Army's work in Coventry earlier that year. All over the country, even in the days of the Christian

Mission, folk were using an assortment of flags to head their processions. Now the same yellow, red and blue design would be used everywhere.

'The *crimson* represents the precious blood of Jesus, by which we are all redeemed,' explained Catherine, pointing to the new Coventry flag. 'The *blue* is God's chosen emblem of purity. The *yellow* represents the light and fire of the Holy Spirit; and the *motto*, "Blood and Fire", also reminds us of the blood of Jesus and the fire of the Holy Spirit.'

Mrs. Reynolds, who received the flag on behalf of the Coventry Corps, was a remarkable woman, one of the first 'Hallelujah Lasses'. In the face of difficulties which, as Railton pointed out to Bramwell, 'would have driven most men out of the place in a fortnight,' she had struggled to gain a footing for the Mission in Coventry. Small wonder, then, that when William had determined The Salvation Army should open fire on his home town of Nottingham in 1879, he said to Catherine: 'We'll send Carrie Reynolds!'

'Who will you send with her, William?' questioned Catherine.

'How about "Happy Eliza"?' he answered, his eyes twinkling.

Lieutenant Eliza Haynes had the kind of ready-for-anything spirit on which the early-day Army thrived. After two hard weeks in Nottingham, when not even the usual startling posters had managed to draw a crowd to hear the good news of Jesus Christ, Mrs. Reynolds said to Eliza in great perplexity: 'What shall we do?'

'We must go to our knees!' replied her Lieutenant.

From a quiet night of prayer, Eliza dashed out on a whirlwind tour of the town. Goosegate, Kid Street, Broad Street, the Market Place — all William's old haunts were treated to a vision, the like of which had never been seen since the conversion of Besom Jack.

With 'Happy Eliza' written on streamers floating from her long hair, and 'I am Happy Eliza!' scrawled on a placard across her back, she marched through the streets of Nottingham, shouting invitations to the meetings. The hall was quickly filled, scores of the most desperate characters were saved, and Happy Eliza was soon marching backwards through those same streets, waving a fiddlestick and leading a procession of converted ruffians in singing Railton's words (to the tune 'Marching through Georgia'):

"Shout aloud Salvation boys!
We'll have another song!
 Sing it with a spirit that will start the
  world along;
 Sing it as our fathers sang it
  many a million strong,
 As they went marching to Glory!'

Happy Eliza became a household name. Music-hall songs were written about her; dolls and toys were called after her. Eleven-year-old Lucy Booth came running home in high delight one day to report that in the sweet shop she had heard a street urchin asking for 'a 'aporth of 'appy 'Lizas!' and Katie and Emma, well-known in the Hackney dis-

On active service in Marylebone

trict for their Salvationism, often had ''Appy
Eliza!' called out after them as they passed through
the streets.

From Nottingham William sent Mrs. Reynolds
to begin the Army's work in Ireland in the spring of

1880, while Eliza, now promoted to the rank of Captain, was appointed to open fire on the Marylebone district of London. Hiring a horse-drawn carriage, she plastered it with announcements that Happy Eliza had arrived; then mounting the box-seat with a fiddle, she drove through the streets, a bass-drummer on the roof, and another Salvationist distributing thousands of invitations to the meeting from inside the carriage. The old theatre which had been taken for the occasion was filled with three thousand for her first meeting, and many there were who started upon a new life with Christ because of Eliza's ministry in the West of London.

Uniforms were beginning to be worn by all officers (leaders) and most soldiers (members).

A month after Happy Eliza opened fire in Marylebone, twenty-year-old Emma became responsible for the training of the first batch of women Salvationists to become officers. Her mother, on meeting them, said: 'We must really do something about their hats, Emma. They don't look very "uniform".'

Collecting together several black straw bonnet shapes and, with Emma as her model, Catherine set about designing the first 'Hallelujah bonnet'.

On June 16, 1880, twenty-five women cadets under Emma's care marched from Hackney to Whitechapel for the public silver wedding celebration of William and Catherine. This was the first appearance of the new bonnets — neat, distinctive and uniform. Very soon they were to prove a useful means of protection as well.

18

ONWARD TO CONQUER THE WORLD

'JESUS WAS BORN in a stable! If that was good enough for Him, this will do well for the birthplace of The Salvation Army in America!' exclaimed young Eliza Shirley as she stood between her parents in a disused Philadelphia chair factory which was now half forge, half stable, and with a horse tied up in one corner.

Joining the Coventry Corps soon after Captain Mrs. Carrie Reynolds commenced Army work there, Eliza became an officer at sixteen and then obtained permission from the General to emigrate with her parents to America in 1879 to attempt to start the Army there.

'If it is a success we may see our way to take it over,' William had written to her characteristically.

It *was* a success; such a success, in fact, that only four months later, in 1880, Railton and seven Hallelujah lasses set sail for New York to take part in the Army's first official overseas invasion. Among the great crowd of Salvationists who gathered at

Tidal Basin, Tilbury, to see them off on that wet February morning was Eva Booth, now aged fourteen. She had a special interest in the occasion, for not only was Railton (the Booth's beloved 'lodger') leading the American invasion, but Emma Westbrook was one of the seven Hallelujah lasses accompanying him.

As she watched red-headed Emma smiling through her tears while Mama bade her farewell, Eva's mind went back to her childhood days, with Emma the devoted cook of the Booth household. On one occasion Eva and Marian were busy at their lessons, when Marian, never able to study much since her smallpox attack, so infuriated the governess by her slowness, that that lady took hold of the child's beautiful hair and pulled her head first one way and then the other. Recalling the verse from the Bible that Mama often quoted to her children, 'Whatsoever thy hand findeth to do, do it with thy might,' Eva shot out her small hand and slapped the cheek of the governess as hard as she possibly could.

'Go straight to bed, you wicked child!' the governess ordered, 'and no lunch or supper shall you have — nothing but dry bread and a glass of milk.'

Mama had been away from home at the time, Eva remembered, as she stood on the station watching Emma talking now with Mama. That dear redheaded cook had insisted Mama would never have punished her headstrong daughter by loss of food. So after dark, Emma Westbrook stole into Eva's bedroom, with jam tarts hidden under her apron.

'Do you think I should have jam tarts when I'm supposed to have only dry bread?' asked Eva, her conscience troubling her. Conscience or not, the jam tarts were soon disposed of by the hungry culprit.

For two days Eva had refused to say she was sorry. Then Mama had returned. 'It might have been right for you to defend Marie,' Mama had explained. 'But I'm sure you're sorry for the way you did it, aren't you?'

Eva had still wanted to say, 'No', until she caught a certain look in Mama's eyes; so she replied: 'Nearly.'

Long afterwards, when Eva was made Commander of the massively-grown American forces of The Salvation Army, she recalled that morning on the quay-side when red-headed Emma had smiled through her tears, and then she remembered the jam tarts by candlelight and the *nearly* being sorry, and Eva thanked God for Emma Westbrook.

The work of The Salvation Army in Australia was started in 1880 by two Christian Mission converts who had emigrated from different parts of England and met 'by accident' in Adelaide, South Australia. A good many things about the rapidly-spreading Salvation Army seemed to happen 'by accident' in those days.

Railton, passing through Canada on his way back to England from America in 1881, seemed to hear a voice telling him to stop and hold an open-air meeting in a Halifax street. 'By accident' he became so engrossed in telling the crowd the good news of Jesus Christ, that his ship went without him, and he had to wait ten days 'without a scrap of luggage', before the next one sailed. That was no hardship to Railton; it simply provided him with ten more days in which to preach salvation on Canadian soil.

'By accident' a year later, in 1882, two young English immigrants met in another part of Canada and, discovering each other to be Salvationists, began holding open-air meetings immediately. Within two years, the Army's Canadian strength had grown to forty corps and one hundred officers.

The Army's invasion of France, on the other-hand, had *not* happened 'by accident'. 'The world is waiting for you!' Catherine had told Katie when she was just a little girl in socks, and now Katie was to be the first of the family to leave her homeland in the cause of the world's salvation. In 1881, twenty-two-year-old Katie and her two young lieutenants were dedicated for that task in a crowded meeting held in a large hall in London's West End. One of her lieutenants, nineteen-year-old Florence Soper, was one day to become Bramwell's wife.

Presenting to Katie the first French flag, Catherine said: 'Carry it into the slums and alleys, everywhere there are lost and perishing souls, and preach under its shadow the everlasting gospel of Jesus Christ.'

After two weeks of the most bitter fighting against the devil, amidst disturbances and abuse of the worst kind, in one of the most sordid parts of Paris, Katie had still made no convert. Believing and praying and fighting, she and her lieutenants went on, and at last the tide of battle turned.

The beginning of what proved to be a memorable meeting was more than usually unpromising. One of the tormentors, a terrible woman, known locally as 'the devil's wife', excelled herself that night. Of immense size, she used to stand in the meeting hall her arms akimbo and sleeves rolled up above the elbows; with one wink she would set everybody screaming and yelling.

During this particular meeting there was not a thing that Katie and her lieutenants did or said that 'the devil's wife' did not turn to ridicule. The fun grew so fast and furious that some of the audience began to dance. The meeting seemed lost; but, by a master-stroke, Katie turned defeat into victory.

Through the din she shouted: 'Mes amis! I will give you twenty minutes to dance, if you will then give me twenty minutes to speak. Are you agreed?'

The tall, dark, handsome ringleader of the disturbance jumped up and said: 'Citizens, it is only fair play!' and they all agreed. They had their dance, and at the end of twenty minutes the ringleader, standing with watch in hand, cried: 'Time up, citizens; it is *la Capitaine's* turn!'

Keeping the bargain, everybody sat down, and an extraordinary silence filled the hall. Not for a mere twenty minutes, but for an hour and twenty minutes Katie held the meeting spellbound.

After the audience had filed out, Katie noticed the ringleader sitting silently at the back of the hall, like a statue.

'Thank you,' she said, as she went down to him. 'You've helped me tonight. Have you understood what I've been saying?'

'I believe that *you* believe what you say.'

'Oh! of course *I* believe.'

With a sigh he asked: 'Have you time to listen?'

'Yes, certainly,' Katie replied quietly.

It was midnight and they were alone in the large hall as he began to tell his story.

'I had the happiest home in Paris. I married the woman I loved, and after twelve months a little boy came to our home. Three weeks later my wife lost her reason, and now she is in an asylum. But there was still my little boy. He was a beautiful child. We ate together, slept together, walked and talked together. He was all the world to me ... This went on until his sixth year and then ...' His lips trembled and he buried his face in his hands.

'He died,' Katie said softly.

Smothering a groan, the man continued: 'And then I went to the devil. At the child's grave in the cemetery I lifted my hand to heaven and cried: "If there be a God, let Him strike me dead!"'

'But He didn't strike you dead.'

'No.'

'He is very gentle and patient with us all. And now you have come here tonight. Doesn't it seem strange to you that *you* out of all the millions in

France, and *I* out of all the millions in England, should be all alone together here at midnight? How do you account for it? Isn't it because God thought of you and loves you? ... Do you ever pray?'

'I pray? Never!'

'But *I* pray,' said Katie, and kneeling down she prayed fervently for his salvation from sin. When she opened her eyes the tears were coursing down his face 'like rain', she thought, remembering the long-ago telling of the story about Mama and her drunkard at Gateshead. She knew the Frenchman's heart was melted, and she spoke to him of the love of God.

'But I have hated Him. I have hated religion; I have come here to mock you ...'

'Yet God loves you.'

'But why did He allow my wife to lose her reason and my child to die, if He loves me?'

'I can't answer those questions,' Katie said earnestly. 'You will know one day. But I *know* He loves you.'

'Is it possible that He can forgive me?'

'It is certain,' answered the second Catherine Booth with joy; her first French convert was being won for God.

One night afterwards, Emile stood up in the crowded meeting hall and gave his testimony, and from that day forward he became one of Katie's best helpers.

Then, in the winter of 1882, twenty months after having established The Salvation Army in France, Katie moved on to invade 'lovely Switzerland'.

19

GET YOUR PHOTOGRAPHS
TAKEN!

THE DAY AFTER Katie's twenty-fifth birthday in
September 1883, Catherine wrote: 'My precious
child, words cannot convey what I have suffered
about you during the last twenty-four hours, only
hearing that you were in prison and not knowing
whether anyone was with you, or how you were
being treated . . .'

'Lovely Switzerland' was proving to be
thoroughly inhospitable to The Salvation Army in
general and the second Catherine Booth in particular. Nine months after the Army's first meeting
on Swiss soil, having made hundreds of its citizens
into Salvationists, Katie found herself in
Neuchâtel prison awaiting trial for preaching the
good news of Jesus Christ. Her greatest crime seems
to have been that she was a woman.

Twelve days of imprisonment in a filthy cell were
followed by a two-day trial resulting in Katie's
being set free. As they left the court room, Katie
and her soldiers were roughly handled by the waiting mob; but, so happy were they, they hardly no-

ticed the cuffs and kicks and stones. Though the fighting continued to be rough, within ten years Switzerland was glad that the Salvationists had stayed.

Back home in England, too, opposition to The Salvation Army was mounting fast. In the year 1881–1882, more than 660 Salvationists were injured, and eighty-six, including fifteen women, were sent to prison as a result of witnessing in the open-air. Almost everywhere the Army appeared, rioting followed.

'You know what this is all about, don't you?' said Catherine to fourteen-year-old Lucy, who had been disturbed by the fact that not only Katie, but Ballington, also, had spent some time in prison; and only a few days before, Eva, leading an open-air meeting at Hackney, had been arrested by a policeman.

'Tell me, Mama!' pleaded Lucy.

'Well, darling, we have thousands of converted drunkards in the Army,' Catherine explained, 'who for years spent their money at the public houses. Some of these places, that used to do a roaring trade, are now on the verge of ruin because of our influence. Their publicans bribe customers to create disturbances at our gatherings, so that Salvationists will be arrested as disturbers of the peace.'

Ballington, as it happened, spent only twenty-four hours in Manchester's Belle Vue jail, and was not at all pleased when someone paid his fine and he found himself quickly freed. But in 1882 news reached him from Weston-super-Mare bringing cheer to his heart.

A 'Skeleton Army' had been organized by the brewers and the publicans to provide fierce opposition to The Salvation Army there, as in many other places, and Bill, Ballington's Bethnal Green convert, now commanding the Army's operations in that sea-side town, was at the centre of the fighting. The Skeleton Army time and again attempted to break up the open-air witness of the Salvationists; and very violent they were about it, too! The magistrates decided to take action by demanding that the Salvationists keep off the streets for a year.

When Little Bill refused to suffer such defeat in face of the opposition, he was arrested and sentenced to three months' imprisonment in Shepton Mallet jail. However, at the end of the sentence a higher court decided that Little Bill, formerly of the Bethnal Green public houses, and now of the Army of Salvation, be allowed to lead as many ex-drunkards and others as he could induce to follow him, in singing about Jesus through the streets of any town he chose. Reading about it in *The Times*, Ballington's heart thrilled with pride at the courage of his brave and faithful convert.

Earlier that year, William and Catherine had themselves been involved in a serious riot in the city of Sheffield. One Sunday morning Salvationists had chalked the pavements with announcements of a huge procession General and Mrs. Booth were to lead through the city the following afternoon.

Consequently a great crowd gathered to see the soldiers march, and amongst the crowd were a good many hooligans, there for a bit of fun.

God's chimney-sweep, Elijah Cadman, arranged the procession with a wagon in front containing that newest of Army novelties, a brass band. This was followed by the converted champion wrestler of Northumberland, mounted on a white horse, who, in turn, was followed by an open carriage in which were William and Catherine. Behind marched the soldiers. No sooner had they got under way than the hooligans pitched in.

The brass band was mobbed and pelted, though the converted wrestler on his white charger was prime target. Plastered with mud and knocked insensible with stones and other objects, he would have fallen from his horse, had not hooligans on either side pulled so hard at both his legs at the same time, that he stayed mounted until the hall was reached. As he was carried to hospital, almost insensible with pain, he whispered: 'I hope they'll get saved.'

Standing in the open carriage, William, for the second time in his life, became an ideal moving target, but miraculously he escaped unhurt.

Battered and bleeding and covered with mud, the valiant Salvationists eventually reached the hall where their meeting was to be held.

'Now is the time to get your photographs taken!' William said, proudly surveying his dishevelled and wounded troops.

The sight upon the platform was unique. Bruised

The brass band leads the procession

and bandaged heads, faces gashed with stones, clothes daubed with blood and mud, and *joy* beaming from every one of those brave Salvationists.

'And you, Mama? What happened to you? Did the hooligans hurt you?' questioned Lucy, wide-eyed, on her parents' return.

'Oh, I only got a botch of mortar on my bonnet,' Mama smiled, remembering. 'I felt quite sorry to have to wash it off the next morning. Those Hallelujah bonnets are certainly proving an excellent means of protection in the thick of the fight. Hurry up and get ready to wear one, Lucy!'

Nearer home, the younger members of the Booth family were becoming more and more familiar with such opposition. No longer did it horrify Lucy, for she was learning quickly that out of the most fearful fighting the best converts were often won. Take Charles Jeffries, for instance. Lieutenant of the Whitechapel Skeleton Army at seventeen, he had attracted to himself a group of like-minded lads, bent at all costs on driving the local Salvationists off the streets. With cap-bands bearing the title Skeleton Army, and carrying a skull and crossbones banner in imitation of the Salvationists' banner of blood and fire, they had time and again upset the open-air witness of the Salvationists.

One New Year's Day Lucy decided to attend the evening meeting at Whitechapel, where Bramwell was to be the preacher. The open-air gathering had been held as usual outside the Blind Beggar public house but, as the time for the indoor meeting drew nearer, there was no sign of the procession arriving. Leaving her seat in the hall, Lucy went to the door to see where they were. As she peered out into the frosty night a strange sight met her eyes. There, at the front of the Salvationists, the Skeleton Army was shuffling along, headed by Jeffries, perched on the shoulders of a Salvationist wearing a high top hat with a Salvation Army ribbon round it. Eva, who at fifteen had recently acquired her first uniform and bonnet, was in the march with the Salvationists, and later, in high delight, described to Lucy how this state of affairs had come about.

'We finished the open-air meeting and were lining up to march back here, when the Skeletons got in front of us and crept at such a snail's pace that we were forced to do the same; and all the while they jostled and pelted us with decayed fruit and mud from the gutters.' (Here Eva stopped to brush some of that same mud off her long, navy-blue skirt.)

'Well, noticing our high-hatted comrade in the front rank, Jeffries leapt upon his shoulders and pushed the hat over his eyes. Then he did no more than use the top hat as a drum and his legs as a goad to drive the poor man to the hall. Oh, Lucy, it looked so funny!' Eva giggled, at the same time making sure that none of her comrades heard her. 'We could only have dismounted Jeffries by rolling Mr. High-Hat in the mud!'

Taking their seats, the girls noticed that several of the Skeletons had actually come into the hall, headed by Jeffries, only to find that all the seats were filled, except those on the front row. Down they sat, expecting to have fun. As Captain Baugh and Bramwell arrived on the platform to commence the meeting, Mrs. Baugh, the Captain's wife, came in from the back of the hall with her young baby, and finding that the only available place was in the middle of the front row, she joined the Skeletons!

'That was the best thing that could have happened!' Eva told Bramwell afterwards. 'The hooligans were so intent on amusing the baby, that they forgot to disturb the meeting.'

'Yes, but even so, when Jeffries knelt at the Penitent-form during the prayer meeting, everyone thought he was playing the fool,' remembered Lucy.

Quietly, Bramwell said: 'I could see his face; I could see his tears.'

And in the Booth household that New Year's night there was great rejoicing for yet another of the enemy won for the Lord.

20

I SHALL COME PROGGING ABOUT

FOUR WEDDINGS AND several years later, William and Catherine's family had grown to include doctor's daughter, Florence Soper (whom Bramwell married in 1882); vicar's daughter, Maud Charlesworth (whom Ballington married in 1886); one-time Quaker businessman, Arthur Clibborn (who married Katie in 1887); and Frederick de Latour Tucker, lately of the Indian Civil Service (who married Emma in 1888). Each was an officer in The Salvation Army, and each of their marriages had been conducted by William.

By the time of Emma's wedding to the pioneer of Army work in India, all William and Catherine's remaining children (except frail Marian) were also involved as officers in the Army. By that time, too, the family knew, with sorrow, that it would not be long before Catherine ceased her warfare and went to heaven.

During her life Catherine had experienced a very great deal of illness. Now, at fifty-nine, it had become necessary for her to visit a specialist. At her own insistence, she went alone; and alone she heard that there was little hope of her recovering.

'How long, then, am I likely to live?' she heard herself ask; and alone she heard the answer: 'At the utmost two years.'

Kneeling on the floor of the horse-drawn cab that sped her towards home and William, Catherine poured out the 'unutterable yearnings' of her soul to God.

William, due to leave for Holland that very evening, saw the cab arriving and bounded down the steps to meet her. She smiled through her tears at him as he helped her up the steps and, trembling with the knowledge of what it would cost him to hear it, she gradually unfolded the fearful news.

Speechless, William sat down, as his love, his precious Kate, came and knelt beside him, saying: 'Do you know what was my first thought?' Their eyes looked long into each others. 'That I should not be there to nurse *you* in your last hour.'

William told Bramwell later that evening: 'She talked ... like an angel to me; she talked as she had never talked before, I could say little or nothing ... I could only kneel with her and try to pray.'

To the Netherlands William went on that chill February night, for Catherine had resolved, no matter what the cost, the fight for the world's salvation must go on.

Apart from Emma's marriage, Catherine found strength to speak in public on only three occasions after that, the final one being to a vast congregation at London's famous City Temple. Then, in a state of collapse, she was driven home, never to mount pulpit or platform again.

But, from the house at Clacton-on-Sea where she was taken to rest and wait, her ministry continued. Letter upon letter was dictated to her family, to her friends, to her Army 'children' (for Catherine had long been known as 'the Army Mother'). Delegation upon delegation of Salvationists came to her room, to receive her blessing and bring their love. Conference upon conference was held at her bedside by William and Bramwell and Railton, for Catherine's wisdom and logic and vision could scarcely be dispensed with even now.

Ballington and Maud brought their baby son from the U.S.A. to see Grandmama; Emma returned from India to be with her; Lucy became her mother's constant companion; and always Catherine thought beyond herself to others. 'Eva, don't forget that man with handcuffs on. Find him. Go to Lancaster jail ... Tell him your mother prayed, when she was dying, for him, and that she had a feeling in her heart that God would save him.'

One night when Catherine was alone with William, she took hold of his hand. Then, slipping the ring off her finger, and on to his, she said: 'By this token we were united for time, and by it now we are united for eternity.'

On Katie's birthday in 1890, the fifth family wedding was celebrated: Herbert's to Dutch military officer's daughter, Cornelie Schoch. She, too, was a Salvation Army officer. Catherine, very near to heaven now, could not be part of their joy.

On the evening of Friday, October 3, her family gathered round her bed for the last time, singing the old hymns of her Methodist beginnings and the well-loved songs of her Army continuings. As a storm-tossed sea raged beyond the windows, inside her room the family lifted their voices in Herbert's chorus:

> 'Victory for me
> Through the blood of Christ my Saviour!
> Victory for me
> Through the precious blood!'

'Lord — let the end be easy — for Emma's sake,' prayed Catherine; and her prayer was answered, as the morning dawned on her last hours upon earth. That afternoon — Saturday, October 4 — Catherine Booth went to heaven.

'Never think of me as in the grave,' she had told her family.

'I shall get about, you may depend. I have in this world, and I shall in the next . . .

'I don't believe I shall be fastened up in a corner playing a harp. I shall let the folks do it who like; but I shall come progging about if I can. I shall come progging about . . .'

21

WHEN THE GENERAL'S DREAM
COMES TRUE

'Do you know, Cousin Gregory, I saw little children crying — for bread — in Kid Street the other day?' William had said as a boy of thirteen, aghast at the misery he had seen in the slums of Nottingham.

'Do you know, Bramwell, that fellows are sleeping out at night on the bridges? Sleeping out all night on the stone?' said William forty-five years later, aghast at the sights he had seen as he crossed the Thames late one bitter winter's night.

'Yes, General,' Bramwell replied, adding, 'didn't you know that?'

'You *knew* that,' William said incredulously, 'and you haven't done anything? Go and *do something! Do something,* Bramwell, *do* something!'

As Bramwell made for the door, all set to obey that command, William shouted after him: 'Get a shed for them; anything will be better than nothing, a roof over their heads, walls round their bodies; you needn't pamper them!'

Immediately Shelter and Food Depôts were set

up in 1888, they were besieged by more homeless people than the Army had room to house, and more hungry people than they had food to feed. Money was desperately needed for the work. There could be no question now of Catherine's appealing to vast and wealthy audiences to support William's work with their donations; he must find some other way.

'I'll write a book!' he decided, and write a book he *did*, spending many a long hour in the next two years, from 1888 to 1890, sitting beside the bed of his dying Catherine, writing.

When the book was finished it needed a title. *In Darkest Africa* was the name of another recently-published and widely-read volume. What about 'Darkest England'? People required their attention to be drawn to that.

'Every *cab-horse* in London has three things,' he wrote. 'A shelter for the night, food for its stomach, and work allotted to it by which it can earn its corn ... When he is down he is helped up, and while he lives he has food, shelter and work.'

What of the 'Submerged Tenth' of the population, the poor of the land, men and women and boys and girls who had *no* such rights? Were they not of more value to God than many cab-horses? It was for *them* that William's social scheme had been devised, the culmination of a dream he had had whilst straddling the workbench of his cousin's tiny Nottingham shop, years before. Publishing this dream just after Catherine's death in 1890, and hard on the heels of H. M. Stanley's *In Darkest*

A queue of hungry people outside a Shelter and Food Depôt

Africa, he called it, *In Darkest England and the Way Out*.

The 'Way Out' of 'Darkest England', as William dreamed it, was to be achieved not only by providing shelter and food for the homeless, but by providing them also with work, and with training for that work, so that they might become thoroughly self-supporting and self-respecting, perhaps for the first time in their lives. So it was that The Salvation Army opened the first employment exchange in Britain, twenty-three years before the Government followed its example! An emigration scheme was commenced, so that folk who could not find work in England might, with new hope, start a new life in a new land.

When William, due to the popularity of his book, was still 'the most talked-about man in Britain', he opened a match-making factory. Matches in those days were made of phosphorus, a poison which found its way into the jawbone of many a worker, causing 'phossy jaw' and certain death. The Army's factory was clean, light, well-aired, and produced only safety matches. Wages were increased by a third of the usual match-making rates, and tea-breaks were plentiful. The public were encouraged to 'worry their oilman, or shopkeeper, who does not at present stock or sell those matches, at least twice a week, until such time as he shall do so'. Then, when other factories began to adopt similar standards, the Army turned its attention to further social evils.

Another popular Salvation Army ballad at that time included these verses:

> Oh, the General's dream, that noble scheme,
> Gives John Jones work to do;
> He'll have a bed and be well fed,
> When the General's dream comes true.
>
> For the hungry, starving, homeless wrecks
> Abounding everywhere,
> This scheme allows that either sex
> Shall have a cab-horse fare:
> The cab-horse has its work, you'll find,
> With food and shelter too;
> Man shall no longer be behind,
> When the General's dream comes true.
>
> When a cab-horse falls upon the street,
> No matter who's to blame,
> If carelessly he missed his feet,
> They lift him just the same.
> The sunken of our fallen race –
> A tenth is not a few –
> We'll lift them up in every case,
> When the General's dream comes true.

Above all, William insisted, the 'Way Out' of 'Darkest England' was to be found not merely in a new outfit of clothes, or enough food to eat, or even in better living conditions; these things were all outside a person, and if the *inside* remained unchanged, the whole scheme would prove useless.

No! the 'Way Out' of 'Darkest England' was to

be found only in every man, woman and child experiencing a heart-changing encounter with God, so that *His* purposes might be let loose in His world. Then, and only then, William realized, would the General's dream come true.

22

ONLY ONE AMBITION

'You can only keep company with God,' William once said, 'by running at full speed;' and in the final twenty years of his life he was still running as strongly as ever. His social schemes for the poor had turned the public spotlight on the Army as never before, and though there was still criticism of its methods, and prosecutions resulting from its persistent open-air witnessing, the fierce and brutal persecution of the 1880s had long since died down.

'There aren't any more Skeletons left to convert,' the world mused affectionately, 'so now he begins on Royalty!' It did seem that everybody who was anybody appeared anxious to meet the ageing General of The Salvation Army.

Much of William's time in those years was spent in visiting the fifty-eight countries in which the Army flag was proudly flying; and wherever he went, great receptions were held in his honour, prime ministers, kings and emperors received him courteously, and ordinary folk flocked to hear him gladly.

Whether in audience with Edward VII at Buckingham Palace, or in company with a group of factory workers who had turned out to greet him as he passed through towns or country lanes on one of his several motorcades, his ambition was always the same. Not for long had his teenage ambition to be 'something great' remained with him, for God had inspired him with a finer ambition — the souls of men.

In King Edward's autograph album William had written:

> Some men's ambition is art,
> Some men's ambition is fame,
> Some men's ambition is gold,
> My ambition is the souls of men.

It was an ambition that, for seventy years, drove William into undreamed-of situations.

One day, for instance, William had accompanied Lord Loch and Cecil Rhodes (after whom Rhodesia was named) to the Army's Farm Colony at Hadleigh in Essex, a notable part of the General's Darkest England Scheme. Both the great men were deeply interested and immensely impressed by what they saw; William's mind was busy about his 'ambition'. In the railway carriage on the way back to London, he put his hand on Cecil Rhodes' arm and said: 'I want to speak to you about yourself. You're a man with much depending on you just now. Tell me, how is it with your soul?'

At this, Lord Loch, who was also travelling with them, looked thoroughly surprised, but Cecil

Rhodes answered immediately: 'Well, General, it's not quite so well with my soul as I could wish.'

'Do you pray?' enquired William.

'Sometimes; not quite as often as I should.'

'Will you let me pray with you — now?'

'Yes.'

Lord Loch turned his eyes away and gazed out of the window. His two travelling companions knelt down, there and then, in the railway compartment and William talked to God on behalf of the mighty Rhodes.

Rising from their knees, Rhodes took William's hand and said: 'I hope you will continue to pray for me.'

And William did; how could he fail to, he whose ambition was the souls of men?

In the springtime of 1912, at a vast public gathering in London's Royal Albert Hall, William Booth told his audience: 'I am going into dry-dock for repairs.'

At eighty-three he was almost blind; nevertheless, his words echoed round that mighty hall as he declared:

'While women weep, as they do now, I'll fight; while little children go hungry, as they do now, I'll fight; while men go to prison, in and out, in and out, as they do now, I'll fight; while there is a drunkard left, while there is a poor lost girl upon the streets, while there remains one dark soul without the light of God, I'll fight — I'll fight to the very end!'

And he did. Very near to the end of that fight,

Bramwell was summoned to the room of the General whose fighting ambition had for so long been the souls of men.

'Bramwell, I want you to promise me that when my voice is silent and I am gone from you, you will ... do more for the homeless of the world. The homeless men. Mind! I am not thinking of this country only, but of all the lands.'

'Yes, General, I understand.'

'The homeless women. Ah, my boy, we don't know what it means to be without a home.'

'Yes, General, I follow.'

'The homeless children. Oh, the children! Bramwell, *look after the homeless*. Promise me.'

When the promise had been given, William exclaimed with a touch of his old humour: 'Mind! If you don't, I shall come back and haunt you!'

The General was 'promoted to Glory' on August 20, 1912, and Lucy, sitting waiting during her father's half conscious moments as he was slipping from her, heard him say: 'Oh, to save these people! ...' And then he was counting again, just as he had lain in bed when he was a boy, counting the strokes of the church clock that didn't know how to strike thirteen. Now, it was not clock strokes he was counting, it was souls; seeking souls; struggling souls; souls growing strong in the strength of the Lord their God.

Had not his ambition always been the souls of men?

BOOKS TO READ

to find out more about
William and Catherine Booth
and The Salvation Army.

The General Next to God, by Richard Collier (Collins)
A Hundred Years' War, by Bernard Watson
(Hodder and Stoughton)
The History of The Salvation Army (5 Vols.), by Robert
Sandall and Arch R. Wiggins (Nelson) and (Vol. 6) by
Frederick Coutts (Hodder and Stoughton)
Blood and Fire! by Edward Bishop (Longmans)
The Young William Booth, by Bernard Watson
(Max Parrish)
Catherine Booth, by Catherine Bramwell Booth
(Hodder and Stoughton)
Social Evils the Army has Challenged by S. C. Gauntlett
(S. P. & S. Ltd.)
My Best Men are Women, by Flora Larsson (Hodder and
Stoughton)

All these books and many others are
obtainable from:

Salvationist Publishing and Supplies Ltd.,
117–121 Judd Street,
London WC1H 9NN

or from your local library.

Army Without Guns, by Cyril Barnes
and a number of useful pamphlets can
be obtained from:

Salvation Army Information Services,
101 Queen Victoria Street,
London EC4P 4EP.